GUY MOTORS

BUSES AND COACHES

GUY MOTORS
BUSES AND COACHES

KEVIN WARRINGTON

THE CROWOOD PRESS

First published in 2018 by
The Crowood Press Ltd
Ramsbury, Marlborough
Wiltshire SN8 2HR

www.crowood.com

British Library Cataloguing-in-Publication Data
A catalogue record for this book is available from the British Library.

ISBN 978 1 78500 497 1

Typeset by D & N Publishing, Baydon, Wiltshire

Printed and bound in India by Parksons Graphics

CONTENTS

Acknowledgements 6

Preface 7

Chapter 1 GUY MOTORS LIMITED: THE BEGINNING 8

Chapter 2 GROWTH AND EXPANSION IN THE 1920s 15

Chapter 3 GUY TROLLEYBUSES 37

Chapter 4 THE 1930s – TROUBLED TIMES AND UTILITY VEHICLES 45

Chapter 5 POST-WAR EXPANSION 64

Chapter 6 REPOSITIONING THE ENGINE AND THE NEW ARAB IV 85

Chapter 7 UTILITIES REBUILT AND VARIATIONS ON A THEME 105

Chapter 8 OTTERS, VIXENS, WARRIORS AND VICTORIES 117

Chapter 9 WULFRUNIAN – TOO MUCH TOO SOON? 135

Chapter 10 THE BEGINNING OF THE END 155

Chapter 11 GUYS IN PRESERVATION 172

Index 206

ACKNOWLEDGEMENTS

Creating this book would never have been possible without help from many enthusiasts, who have given their time to create extensive fleet lists of vehicles that are published on the Internet and have been extremely helpful for confirming both dates in and out of service and helping to verify details such as the origins of bodies fitted. The resources compiled by The PSV Circle have proved invaluable as a thoroughly reliable source of information and I have also used with gratitude the lists created by Peter Gould and buslistsontheweb.co.uk. Without these valuable online resources, checking information would have been so much more difficult and time-consuming. Similarly, the archive of the magazine *Commercial Motor* has proved to be of great value, not just from the position of confirming technical data, but also in forming a view of how the output of Guy Motors was considered when newly introduced.

In the research for the book, I've had the pleasure of visiting many of the collections of preserved vehicles in the United Kingdom, where the custodians have without exception been unfailing in their help. In particular, I would like to thank everyone involved with the museums at Aldridge (formerly the Aston Manor Road Transport Museum), Wythall, Dewsbury and Lathalmond, who made me welcome during my visits and provided unrestricted access for photography. Whenever I found a Guy vehicle at a rally, the owners were more than willing to chat about their prize possession and help with information as needed.

IMAGES

I've used a variety of sources for images to illustrate this work, aiming to achieve a balance of newly created modern digital photographs of preserved vehicles, most of which are my own work, and historical period images that have been obtained from various archives and collections. The archives of the Online Transport Archive, the Omnibus Society and 1066 online were all exceptionally helpful in providing historical images. Other images have been sourced from various library and local authority archives, the one at Wolverhampton being worthy of a special mention for their assistance. A number of images have been supplied from Wolverhampton City Archives and are reproduced with their permission.

My very good friend and fellow enthusiast, Clive Wilkin, provided many of the images of vehicles in service from the 1950s and 1960s; his contributions are acknowledged with his initials 'CW' in the captions. I must also thank my wife, Ann, as usual, for her patience in helping with this work, especially for proofreading the drafts.

PREFACE

As a young boy at the end of the 1950s, I moved with my parents to a new housing estate built to accommodate the overflowing population of Portsmouth. Bus journeys became a way of life for trips into town to visit family and for other essential social activities, as the development of other facilities lagged far behind the provision of new housing. The bus services were extensive, especially in the morning and afternoon to accommodate the needs of the rehoused residents making their way to and from work, which for the most part remained in the city. Portsmouth Corporation at the time operated a large fleet of almost exclusively Leyland vehicles, smartly finished in a red and white livery. These were augmented on longer routes out of the city by Southdown Motor Services, which again were a predominantly Leyland customer, but did have a few other vehicles that we would see from time to time. Moving slightly further westwards along the coast, we would run into the fleet of Hants & Dorset, exclusively Bristol and Eastern Coach Works of course, and venturing as far as Southampton would bring us to a large fleet of entirely different vehicles that proudly bore the word 'GUY' on their radiators. Although more basic in finish and austere in style, these were impressive vehicles even to a primary school-age child. They seemed to be faster and more powerful than the Portsmouth buses and Southampton had steep hills that the buses would charge up and speed back down again.

Just across Portsmouth Harbour we would encounter the Provincial fleet of green buses. These to my young eyes seemed to be a mixture, but many had the magical word 'GUY' on them and some even had the Indian Chief's Head on the radiator cap. And like so many other young boys, I 'learned' to drive a bus by watching how the real driver did it. When I did eventually learn to drive a half-cab bus with a crash box, I quickly discovered that it isn't *quite* as easy as it appeared and accepted that I might have been just a little harsh as a little boy in my scoring of the driver's abilities to execute clean gear changes.

Moving on to gain engineering qualifications, I developed a fascination for elegant designs, especially those that take a novel approach to a series of problems and provide a solution that on paper should work well, but where the implementation appeared to create more problems than were originally to have been solved.

While the vast majority of Guy's products were simple, robust and workmanlike, one model, far ahead of its time but woefully under-engineered, shines as an example of such a design. This is of course the Wulfrunian.

A similar fascination with railways led me to compare the Wulfrunian with the Merchant Navy class railway locomotives of the Southern Railway; again, the implementation of multiple new designs into a single new class of machine rushed into production before the numerous and inevitable shortcomings in the design had been evaluated and resolved. While these locomotives, with their smaller 'Light Pacific' cousins, went on to provide long service for the nationalized British Railways, the Wulfrunian was to have a catastrophic effect on its manufacturer. With supreme irony, many of the features that were to be pioneered in that design are now taken for granted.

When the opportunity to create a new book on a range of bus and coach models arose, the choice of Guy Motors became an automatic choice.

Chapter 1

GUY MOTORS LIMITED:
THE BEGINNING

Half-cab buses were for many years the traditional form of public transport in the United Kingdom. Now kept at the North West Museum of Road Transport, DFM 347H was the final Guy bus chassis to be delivered for the home market.

Leyland. AEC. Bristol. Bedford. All names that come quickly to mind when considering the companies that made a significant contribution to passenger transport in the twentieth century. Leyland were the leading choice of municipal operators across the country; AEC were synonymous with London Transport, particularly with the RT rear-entrance double-decker, RF single-deck front-entrance bus and of course the Routemaster – the stereotype half-cab rear-entrance double-decker that has become a worldwide symbol for London. Bristol, nearly always with bodywork designed and built by Eastern Coach Works in Lowestoft, was the choice of the nationalized Tilling Group, uniquely available to that undertaking until the market was liberalized and the designs were made available in the general market. Bedford, the commercial vehicle brand of Vauxhall Motors, owned since the 1920s by General Motors, was the lightweight chassis choice of the independent, with single-deck buses and coaches constructed by the likes of Duple and Plaxton on a chassis derived from Bedford's extensive range of goods vehicles.

And Guy Motors. Conventionally designed but with many innovative features, robust and economical to operate with a long service life. So long, that often life-expired bodywork would be removed, scrapped and a new body installed on to the still serviceable chassis. A company that produced motor buses both single and double deck; touring coaches and trolleybuses; and which developed a substantial export market worldwide. Guy's products sold across all markets, the output of a progressive and forward-thinking Wolverhampton-based business. Not just passenger transport, but also goods vehicles, munitions and, for a short period, motor cars. Later in the life of the company, an overambitious sales expansion, coupled with a technically innovative but underdeveloped bus design, would bring down the company, resulting in it being acquired by Jaguar. With the latter's eventual integration into British Leyland, what had once been a fiercely independent company became all-subsumed into the fiasco that was British Leyland.

THE BEGINNINGS OF GUY MOTORS

Sydney Slater Guy was born on 31 October 1884 in Wolverhampton, the son of Isaiah Guy and his wife Emmeline, who are shown in the 1891 Census as living at 51 Beach Road, Sparkhill, a short distance south of Birmingham. The family home, which no longer exists, having been replaced with modern housing, was shared with a general domestic servant, Susan Brown. Isaiah gave his occupation on Census night as 'Commercial Traveller' and the area appears to have been comfortable, as several neighbours also employed general servants and gave occupations such as 'Chief Clerk' and 'Printer's Manager', while Mr Francis Parkes, the immedi-

Sydney Slater Guy, founder, Managing Director and Chairman of the company that bore his name.
WOLVERHAMPTON CITY ARCHIVE

ate neighbour, also described himself as a 'Commercial Traveller'.

Between 1891 and 1901, the family moved to 34 Cambridge Road, King's Norton, which is the address given for the next official census. Emmeline is recorded as being the head of the household, so we must presume that Isaiah was travelling on business. The family has by now grown to include four sons: Sydney, William Ewart, Frank Maurice and Frederick James. A general servant was still employed: Harriet Lane had replaced Susan Brown. King's Norton is located a little further from the city centre of Birmingham and is now in the 'leafy suburbs'. The occupations given by the neighbours of the Guy family suggest that the area was much the same in 1901.

In 1902, Sydney was coming to the end of his education at Birmingham Technical School, where the subjects he had studied included Mathematics, Physics, Chemistry and Electricity and Magnetism, all subjects that would provide a solid foundation for his future career. From here, he was indentured to Belliss and Morcom, where he would complete a three-year apprenticeship.

Having completed his apprenticeship, Sydney Guy took a position as a senior draftsman at the General Electric Company (GEC) at its newly built factory in Witton to the north of Birmingham city centre. GEC was growing rapidly with huge demand for its electrical products, particularly the Osram brand of incandescent lamps, in which it was a market leader. Sydney was not to stay with GEC for long; in 1906 an opportunity arose for a position as Service Manager at the repair department of the Humber Company in Coventry and Sydney Guy now found himself involved in the industry that was to be his future and in due course to bear his name.

Humber, like many of the Coventry-based motor vehicle manufacturers, had its beginnings in bicycles, developing into motorcycles and, eventually, motor cars. Three years later in 1909, Guy was to leave the position at Humber and move to a position in Wolverhampton. Now aged just twenty-four years, this was to be his final position as an employee and his new employer was the Sunbeam Motor Car Company Limited, whose Works were established at Upper Villiers Street. Despite much redevelopment of the city of Wolverhampton in the intervening years, the Sunbeam Works have survived, although now used for different industrial purposes and with part of it Grade II listed.

SYDNEY GUY'S FIRST EMPLOYER

The foundations of Belliss and Morcom were set out by George Belliss in 1862 when he acquired an engineering business situated in Broad Street, Birmingham, from R. Bach and Company and formed a partnership with Joseph Seekings that survived until 1866, after which Belliss traded as G.E. Belliss and Company, moving in 1875 to new and larger premises located alongside the Birmingham Canal in Ledsham Street, Ladywood, an area that remains industrial on the very edge of the recently redeveloped area of Birmingham city centre around Brindley Place.

The second part of the business name came in 1884 when the first-class former Royal Navy steam engineer Alfred Morcom joined as a partner, although the trading name remained as G.E. Belliss & Co. The main business for the firm was the engineering and construction of electrical generating sets comprising a reciprocating steam engine and directly connected dynamo, with the main users being industrial plants, hospitals and waterworks. Morcom's experience of the maritime industry brought new business that was to result in the firm's products providing main power and electrical generation for the Royal Navy's Sharpshooter class of torpedo gunboats.

The name of Belliss and Morcom was adopted formally in 1899, having become a limited company six years earlier. Customers for generating equipment included the municipal undertakings in Bury St Edmunds and Gloucester and the Glasgow Corporation Tramways.

The future career direction for Sydney Guy and his employer reached an interesting point when in 1907 a double-decker bus was built for the London General Omnibus Company, and although Guy was no longer employed at the time of the delivery, it is interesting to consider that it may have planted a seed in his imagination for the future.

Following the end of World War I, Belliss and Morcom produced a series of internal combustion engines, building their own range of diesel engines until the 1930s. The business continued under the same name until 1968, when it merged with W.H. Allen, Sons and Company to create Amalgamated Power Engineering. Just before the merger, however, Belliss and Morcom purchased the Crossley-Premier Engines business from the receiver. Crossley-Premier had been formed by the Crossley Brothers in Manchester, another famous builder of motor buses, that part of the business being eventually acquired by AEC and, like Guy's business long in the future, being subsumed into British Leyland.

The Amalgamated Power business remained until 1981, when it was acquired by Northern Engineering Industries plc (NEI), a business that had been built on well-established firms in the electrical generating industry, including the turbine business originally established by Charles Parsons. NEI was subsequently purchased by Rolls-Royce in 1989. Eventually, the original business would find itself purchased by US-based industrial equipment manufacturer Gardner Denver and the original name resurrected, now supplying a range of oil-free compressors. There is no connection with the Manchester firm of Gardner, renowned builder of the diesel engines that were to provide power to so many of Guy Motors' products.

Guy's appointment was to be as Works Manager, a very senior position for one of such an age and with relatively little experience. It is reported that immediately after his appointment, one of the Board enquired of his age and Guy is said to have responded that as they (the Board of Sunbeam) had already decided to appoint him to the position, his age was immaterial. This was not to be the only occasion on which a degree of youthful arrogance was to be shown: some years later when applying for membership of the Institution of Automobile Engineers, he increased his age by two years when he was appointed as an Associate Member.

The Sunbeam Motor Car Company had been formed in 1905 from a business founded in 1887 by John Marston to manufacture, not surprisingly, bicycles. Joining the newly fledged car company at around the same time was a French car designer, Louis Coatalen, who came to England in 1900 from his home in Brittany after working for renowned French car manufacturers De Dion-Bouton and Panhard et Levassour. He, too, worked for Humber

prior to forming a partnership with William Hillman and eventually moving to Sunbeam. Coatalen was an enthusiastic motor-sport driver, competing in the 1908 Isle of Man Tourist Trophy race with a Hillman-Coatalen car and developing the Sunbeam 12/16 cars that competed at Dieppe in the Coupe de l'Auto for 3-litre cars and took the first three places. Coatalen is credited in coining the expression that 'motor sport improves the breed'. In the years between the two world wars, Sunbeam were to become an important name in motor sport and in world speed-record endeavours. But this was all to occur long after Sydney Guy had departed.

By 1913, Sunbeam were enjoying a successful period, with profits in the region of £200,000, an increase of tenfold since Guy had joined. Notwithstanding an already generous salary of £250 per year, plus a company-supplied car, Guy was of the opinion that he was due a more substantial compensation in return for his contribution to the company's success. The directors were not of the

SUNBEAM – A WEB OF OWNERSHIP

John Marston set up on his own account first as a tinplate manufacturer in 1859 at the age of twenty-three and expanded by purchasing the Works of Edward Perry, his former employer and apprentice-master. As an enthusiastic cyclist, the fashion of the time, Marston quickly established his own cycle business in 1887 at a factory in Wolverhampton that he named Sunbeamland. A limited company was incorporated in 1895 and five years later, the name Sunbeam was registered to designate motor cars to be built by the company, following the first experimental forays into motor cars in 1899. Other models following the general style for veteran cars were to follow until 1905, when the Sunbeam Motor Car Company was formed to focus on the interests of motor car design and construction. This was the concern to which Sydney Guy would be appointed as Works Manager.

It had been planned that Marston's third son, Roland, would succeed his father as Chairman, but he was to die unexpectedly in March 1918, with John Marston himself dying the morning after Roland's funeral. The bicycle and motorcycle business, which had been separated from the car business, were sold to a business consortium that by 1927 was to have formed into Imperial Chemical Industries and, ten years later, the Sunbeam tradename for motorcycles was disposed of to the owners of the Matchless and AJS brands, which in due course sold the name to BSA.

In 1920, the Sunbeam Motor Car Company was bought by the established French motor company, Darracq, which, the previous year, had purchased London-based Clément-Talbot, with each brand retaining its individual identities. The group had three sets of premises from which it operated: Darracq from Suresnes, then a suburb of Paris; Sunbeam in Wolverhampton; and Clément-Talbot in North Kensington, London. Economies of scale were obtained by centralizing administration, purchasing and advertising under the umbrella name of STD Motors Limited.

In common with many other motor businesses, Sunbeam did not survive the depression of the 1930s and went into receivership in 1934. It was purchased out of receivership by the Rootes Brothers, who were busily acquiring other car manufacturers, notably Hillman and Humber.

To complicate matters further, from the late 1920s Sunbeam extended its production of ambulances on car chassis into larger commercial vehicles, particularly motor buses and trolleybuses. The commercial vehicle business also passed to Rootes, who had also recently purchased the Karrier Motors business from Clayton & Co. of Huddersfield. Karrier also produced trolleybuses, production of which moved to Sunbeam, and small petrol-engined commercial vehicles, which moved to Rootes' Commer business in Bedfordshire.

Then, in 1946, Rootes sold Sunbeam Commercial Vehicles to J. Brockhouse & Co., based in West Bromwich, who in 1948 sold the trolleybus business to … Guy Motors Limited.

The Sunbeam name continued to be used as part of the Rootes group, either as Sunbeam-Talbot, then finally as a marque in its own right, designating cars that were essentially higher-performance Hillman models. Rootes were, if nothing else, consummate masters of what has become known as 'badge engineering'.

same opinion and during May 1914, Guy resigned his position with effect from the end of that month. The directors of Sunbeam wished him well in his new position and an agreement was reached whereby the company car would be returned or paid for by the end of August.

GUY MOTORS LIMITED IS BORN

A new business was incorporated on Saturday, 30 May 1914 by Sydney Guy. It was registered as Guy Motors Limited and established with a capital of £50,000 made up of 45,000 ordinary shares and 5,000 deferred shares, all shares having a nominal value of £1. It is hardly credible that the plans were not in Guy's mind prior to his departure from Sunbeam, especially as designs had been drawn up for a 30cwt light lorry and plans were under way for a factory to be constructed in the Fellings Park

area of Wolverhampton. Traditionally, industrial development in the West Midlands, and particularly in the area around Wolverhampton known as the Black Country, had followed the lines initially of the canals and latterly of the railways. With the introduction of motor transport, reliance on railways and canals to bring in raw materials and take out finished goods was diminishing, giving businesses the opportunity to expand into new areas, which today we might refer to as 'green fields'.

THE GUY FAMILY

The 1911 Census shows the Guy family still living at 34 Cambridge Road; 'Father' is still shown as a 'Commercial Traveller in Hardware' and 'Mother' has no occupation shown. Sydney declares his occupation as 'Works Manager – Motor Works'; William Ewart Guy is shown

An internal, early view of the Guy Motors factory showing chassis assembly. WOLVERHAMPTON CITY ARCHIVE

An aerial view believed to date from the early 1950s showing the extent of the Guy Works at Fallings Park. Today, most of the buildings have been removed and replaced with modern light industrial units. WOLVERHAMPTON CITY ARCHIVE

as an 'Engineer's Fitter'; and Frank and Frederick are still at school. It is interesting that the census data now collects information relating to the number of children born to the marriage, and this shows that Isaiah and Emmeline had a total of nine children, five of whom had

sadly died in infancy. The family no longer appear to have a servant living in, although they may have retained the services of a daily maid who resided elsewhere.

Sydney Guy was married in 1923 to Leila Brooks, the second daughter of Buckley and Anna Maria Brooks, who were at the time of the 1911 Census living at The Manor House in the pleasant area of Hale in Cheshire to the south-west of Manchester, now an area much favoured by the affluent. Mr Brooks gives his occupation as 'Brewery Manager' and the family were clearly living very comfortably, employing a governess for the children's education, a domestic servant and a coachman. Anna was originally from Victoria, Australia, and Leila had four siblings – an elder brother and sister, and a younger brother and sister.

William Guy, known usually by his middle name of Ewart, joined the Guy Motors business and eventually became Sales Director, a position he retained until he died in 1954. The two other brothers were to die relatively young, Frank in the service of his country in the trenches of Flanders in 1917 and Fred in 1938.

Sydney and Leila had three children: Hazel Elizabeth Guy; Trevor Maurice Brooks Guy; and Robin Slater Guy. Trevor and Robin were both to become Directors of the family business.

GUY MOTORS EARLY PRODUCTS

The first product to emerge from the Fellings Plant factory was the 30cwt lorry in September of 1914, some four months after Guy terminated his employment at Sunbeam. This vehicle included a number of innovative design features, including a chassis frame constructed from pressed steel, which provided the same strength but with less weight than the rolled channel chassis that was more usual at the time. An engine, clutch and gearbox were assembled into a subframe, which was suspended from the chassis in three locations, giving the chassis more ability to flex without either fracturing itself or the more usual solid engine mounts.

The petrol engine was not manufactured by Guy, but bought in from the Coventry company of White and Poppe, an independent supplier to many of the smaller vehicle constructors. White and Poppe were eventually to be purchased by Dennis Brothers of Guildford in 1919, a company that was to become well known for its manufacture of fire appliances, as well as buses and coaches that would be in competition with Guy's future products, and which will enter the story again in the next chapter. The engine used by Guy was a 4-cylinder side valve. The clutch was of the cone type and the four-speed gearbox was directly driven in third gear, with fourth forming an overdrive. A speed governor was fitted which only operated in fourth gear, restricting the top speed of the vehicle to 30mph (48km/h).

The same chassis formed the basis for the first passenger vehicle to be built by Guy Motors in 1914 and was supplied for service in the West Highlands of Scotland, operating between the railway station at Achnasheen on the line between Kyle of Lochalsh and Inverness and

The earliest vehicles to emerge from the fledgling Guy Motors Works were similar to this 30cwt lorry seen here with a box-type body carrying what appears to be laundry baskets. WOLVERHAMPTON CITY ARCHIVE

The very first Guy passenger vehicle was a postbus that was supplied for service in the West Highlands of Scotland. As well as providing carriage for fourteen passengers, the vehicle also carried the mail in a secure compartment. WOLVERHAMPTON CITY ARCHIVE

Autbea on the northern side of Loch Ewe. This had a capacity to carry fourteen passengers, plus mail in a secure compartment at the rear of the vehicle.

All this was taking place just a few weeks after Great Britain had declared war on Germany on 4 August 1914. Supplies of vehicles were requisitioned for war work and the new Guy factory found itself used for other war contracts. Of these, the most important, particularly in reference to vehicle production, were two aircraft engines that were built in the second half of the conflict to designs by Granville Bradshaw working for the All British Engine Company (ABC Motors Limited). The Wasp was a 7-cylinder radial engine that developed 160bhp and the Dragonfly was a 9-cylinder radial rated at 350bhp. Neither design appears to have been especially successful.

With one cylinder hidden behind the propeller blade, the nine cylinders confirm that this aircraft engine is the Dragonfly assembled as part of the war effort by Guy Motors. WOLVERHAMPTON CITY ARCHIVE

Chapter 2

GROWTH AND EXPANSION
IN THE 1920s

The Armistice in 1918 resulted in a substantial number of former military motor vehicles being disposed of by the Forces, many of which were to find ready ownership with newly demobilized soldiers who had learnt to drive during the conflict and who now saw an opportunity to set up their own haulage businesses. This was also the era of the charabanc, either purpose-built for passenger carriage or an interchangeable body fitted to a goods vehicle frame to allow passengers to be carried when this was more profitable to the operator. These vehicles were

Charabancs provided a popular form of transport prior to the development of the motor coach, seating four or five abreast. This Guy chassis charabanc has a folding roof for weather protection and it looks as though the passengers in the rearmost seats are perched on top of the folded roof. WOLVERHAMPTON CITY ARCHIVE

very basic, with solid tyres, firm springs and wooden bench seating. To improve the quality of the ride, an innovative pneumatic suspension system developed by Holden was fitted experimentally. This simply comprised an air tube mounted between the chassis and the body, but rapid development of pneumatic tyres suitable for commercial vehicles resolved the issue in a more effective manner.

Entering the 1920s saw the general weight of vehicles increase, along with their engine size, with those built by Guy ranging from 2.72 litres to 4.5 litres. At this time, passenger vehicles were still built on lorry chassis, resulting in the floor level being high above the ground, but in 1923 Bournemouth Corporation purchased three chassis that were equipped with 'toast rack' bodies by the local firm of Steane and ran on small, solid-tyred wheels, which gave the vehicles a slightly comical appearance. However, they proved their worth on the short service between the piers at Bournemouth and Boscombe with a further three being acquired the following year, by which

time they had gained the name of 'Promenade Runabouts' with other seaside resorts taking up the idea of running a tourist seafront service. Along the south coast to the east, Portsmouth Corporation had the same idea and commissioned the local coachbuilder, Wadhams in Waterlooville, to build five similar bodies on Guy's J-type chassis for seafront service between the two piers at Southsea, Clarence Pier and South Parade Pier. In the case of the Southsea service, this was to be the instigation of a continuing summer seafront service that was to continue to run regularly long after the municipal operator had disposed of its passenger business.

The 30cwt lorry chassis showed itself to be a useful platform for bus construction, with a seating capacity of up to thirty passengers. The flat chassis required to construct a cargo-carrying body had a serious drawback when used for mounting passenger coachwork, in that the height of the frame above pavement level required the intending passenger to mount two or three

The driver poses alongside his Guy Promenade photographed in St Helen's Parade while operating in Southsea. The small wheels and solid tyres are visible. This service ran along the seafront, a route that was to change little for many years. ALAN LAMBERT COLLECTION

Thundersley and Hadleigh are located a short distance apart in the county of Essex, close to the resort of Southend-on-Sea. The company of Thundersley, Hadleigh & District Motors Ltd was formed in 1915 to carry out the business of manufacturers and dealers in motor cars and, as illustrated here, operated an early example of a Guy bus in the district. THE OMNIBUS SOCIETY

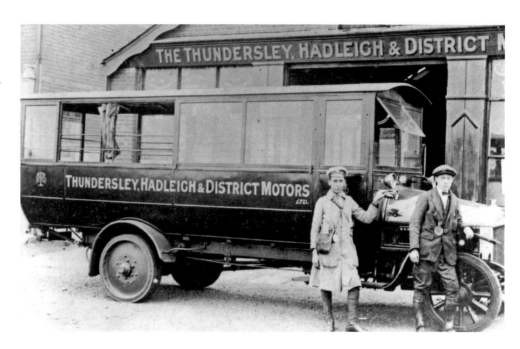

A factory image of a Guy 2.5-ton chassis fitted with a body by Walmer dating from around 1921. NATIONAL MOTOR MUSEUM

steps from ground level to enter the saloon. A solution would be forthcoming in 1924 when Guy introduced the first drop-frame chassis, based around the goods vehicle design, but now allowing much easier access for passengers, who would now need to negotiate just a single step from street level.

GUY VENTURES INTO CARS

Between 1919 and 1925, Guy Motors built a large and upmarket car, powered by a V8 engine of Guy's own design. Copying the lorry design, the engine and gearbox were mounted on a subframe that was isolated from the

Guy Motors produced simple but effective advertising for its products, including this one for the V8-powered car.

chassis using ball joints. The engine had a displacement of 4072cc, was rated at 20HP, and able to achieve a maximum speed of around 80mph (130km/h). A four-speed gearbox, operated by a right-hand positioned lever, was connected to the engine with a cone clutch. Not unusually for the time, the braking system was described as being barely adequate, being rod-operated to the rear wheels only. 1921 brought two smaller models rated at 12HP and 15.9HP, and finally in 1923 the last model of car to be produced by Guy Motors was launched as the 13/36 powered by a 4-cylinder petrol engine with a capacity of 1954cc.

At first glance, this car might appear to be a Rolls-Royce, but it is a 1920 Guy V8 four-door tourer. NATIONAL MOTOR MUSEUM

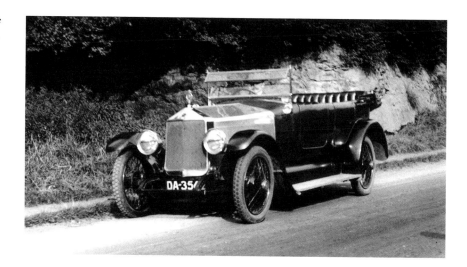

GUY 13/36HP TOURING CAR SPECIFICATION

Layout

Separate pressed-steel frame with either a six-light, four-door saloon body, or four-door tourer, supplied with folding hood and side curtains

Engine

Cylinders — 4-cylinder, in-line

Cooling — Water, film-type radiator, cooling fan driven by engine and circulation by thermo syphon

Bore and stroke — Bore: 2.83in (72mm), stroke: 4.72in (120mm)

Capacity — 1954cc

Valves — 2 valves per cylinder

Fuel supply — Single zenith carburettor, fed from a rear tank via an Autovac

Transmission

Clutch — Leather-faced cone

Gearbox — Four forward speeds and reverse

Suspension and steering

Suspension — Semi-elliptic front and rear with hydraulic dampers to each wheel

Steering — Worm and wheel with adjustable steering column; special note was made that the worm wheel could be fitted in one of four positions to allow for wear

Wheels and tyres

Five detachable artillery wheels supplied as standard, with disc wheels available as an extra-cost option; each wheel fitted with 30 × 3.5 Dunlop Cord tyres

Axles

Front — H section with oil-lubricated kingpins

Rear — Semi-floating, spiral bevel final drive

Electrical system

Dynamo and starting motor; ignition by magneto; electric lighting

Brakes

Type — Foot brake operating by rods to drums on all wheels

Handbrake — Lever operating on rear wheels only

Dimensions

Track — 52in (1,320mm)

Wheelbase — 112.5in (2,857mm)

'FEATHERS IN OUR CAP'

Guy Motors were always well known for their bonnet mascot showing a native American Red Indian head complete with war bonnet. The origin of this was a newspaper advertisement placed in early 1924 boasting of important orders taken in the preceding months, many of which were repeat orders, which, as the copywriters claimed, showed satisfaction in the products. Amongst the customers mentioned, Leeds Corporation, Midland General Omnibus, The War Office, Peek Freans & Co. and Harrods are noted as repeat customers, with each of the thirteen highlighted orders being shown as a feather arranged around a vehicle radiator. The advertising headline shouted 'Feathers in our Cap' and reminded people of the war bonnet worn by Native American warriors and was, in due course, to become the company mascot adorning the radiator cap of many Guy vehicles.

A little newer than the original Guy 'Feathers in our Cap' advertisement, the radiator with a background of feathers, a selection of vehicles produced and a list of repeat customers formed a common theme for Guy's advertising and was widely used in the specialist press.

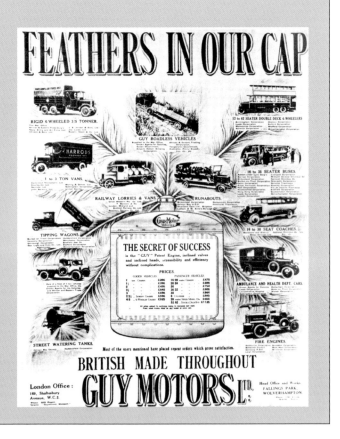

In 1925, the transport undertaking in Wolverhampton obtained its first Guy motor buses, having previously purchased vehicles from Tilling-Stevens. These were two Guy lightweight ¾-ton chassis with thirty-one seat bus coachwork by Fleming, of which number 36 seen here was numerically the first. WOLVERHAMPTON CITY ARCHIVE

The same vehicle seen on an excursion photographed at the Fox Inn at Shipley on the road from Wolverhampton to Bridgnorth, a road that would in the future see many Guy vehicles being tested. The bus had only a short life in its home town, being withdrawn from service after four years. WOLVERHAMPTON CITY ARCHIVE

THE DROP-FRAME CHASSIS

Specifically designed for use as a bus chassis, and the first of the type to be manufactured in Britain, Guy Motors introduced three variations of existing chassis with a dropped centre section of the frame in 1924. Keeping the same designation as the normal height, straight-framed chassis, these were designated as models BA with a wheelbase of 13ft 4in (4,064mm), B with a 15ft 3in (4,648mm) wheelbase and BB with a wheelbase of 16ft 5in (5,004mm). A front or rear entrance could be accommodated, or, for high-density service, a dual entrance could be fitted, although at the cost of a reduced seating capacity. The longest of the three would accommodate up

Reducing the height of the main chassis by creating an arch over the rear axle allowed Guy to introduce the drop-frame chassis, providing for a reduced overall vehicle height and a lower centre of gravity, as well as easing the task of entering the vehicle.

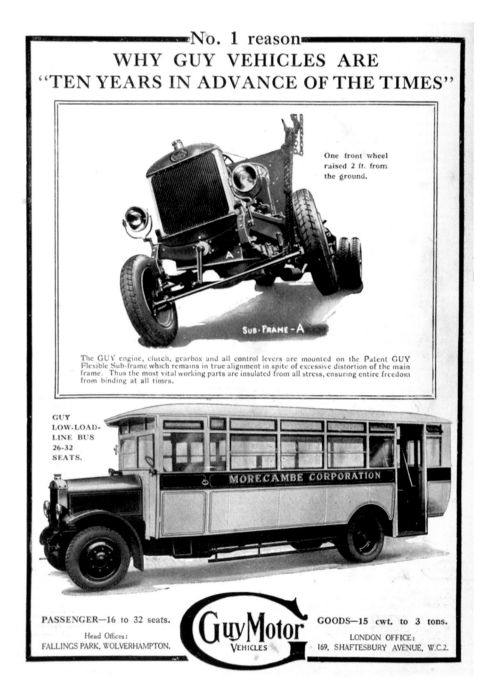

No. 1 reason
WHY GUY VEHICLES ARE
"TEN YEARS IN ADVANCE OF THE TIMES"

One front wheel raised 2 ft. from the ground.

SUB-FRAME - A

The GUY engine, clutch, gearbox and all control levers are mounted on the Patent GUY Flexible Sub-frame which remains in true alignment in spite of excessive distortion of the main frame. Thus the most vital working parts are insulated from all stress, ensuring entire freedom from binding at all times.

GUY LOW-LOAD-LINE BUS 26-32 SEATS.

MORECAMBE CORPORATION

PASSENGER—16 to 32 seats.
Head Offices:
FALLINGS PARK, WOLVERHAMPTON.

Guy Motor VEHICLES

GOODS—15 cwt. to 3 tons.
LONDON OFFICE:
169, SHAFTESBURY AVENUE, W.C.2.

Guy's advertising department liked a good slogan, 'Ten years in advance of the times' being just one that was used to promote the features of the product. This particular advert is believed to have been produced for inclusion in an exhibition catalogue.

Another development came in 1926 with the introduction of the Premier Six model, also referred to as the BK, powered by a 6-cylinder sleeve valve engine developed by Daimler Knight. This new model was extensively reviewed by *Commercial Motor* early in 1926, which gave great emphasis to the ease of maintenance, noting that every assembly on the chassis, other than the wheels of course, could be removed without the need for a lifting jack or pit. The 4-cylinder Guy engine remained available, but the 6-cylinder engine gave a smoother ride and increased torque. Six-cylinder engines had gained much popularity in the United States, where very long distance journeys were more common, and in some of Guy's target export markets, a similar requirement existed.

to thirty passengers. While the advantages of the reduced chassis height were mostly seen by the passenger, drivers were provided with improved handling as a result of the lower centre of gravity. The drop-frame chassis quickly became the standard for bus chassis and was only really superseded more than thirty-five years later with the development of front entrance buses.

At the time the magazine article was produced, Guy had received orders from the city of Rio de Janeiro, following a long and detailed search by that operator in the US and Europe for a suitable vehicle type to meet the city's particular needs. Liverpool Corporation had placed an order for thirty-five single-deck buses built on the chassis and nine for the firm of Keith and Boyle (London)

RIGHT: A late 1920s Guy BB motor coach being operated by Western National on a private hire. The folding canvas roof and drop windows provided an open-air experience for passengers when the weather permitted. THE OMNIBUS SOCIETY

BELOW: Burton-upon-Trent was an exceptionally loyal customer of Guy Motors, purchasing almost exclusively Guy products from its first motor bus in 1926 until 1961, with just a few incursions from other manufacturers. This is a model BB delivered in 1927 with a twenty-five seat bus body built by Guy. THE OMNIBUS SOCIETY

Limited, better known under their trading name as Orange Coaches. The orders received from Rio de Janeiro, which totalled 170 vehicles in 1926, were to prove to be very significant for Guy. Ten years after they were delivered, they were still running in everyday service in 'excellent condition' according to a report by Leyland's Technical Director at that time, who concluded that they would probably still be running in a further ten years' time and that there was little opportunity of business for Leyland in Rio.

Various options were available for braking, either a transmission brake acting on the propeller shaft, with drum brake and expanding shoes on each back wheel, or no transmission brake and twin sets of expanding shoes inside stepped rear brake drums. At the front, Bendix three-shoe brakes were used and a Dewandre servo was available as an option, although its fitting was recommended, as mention was made that despite the brakes having substantial stopping power, to gain maximum efficiency in braking an unassisted vehicle would require significant effort from the driver. A feature of the servo-assisted brakes was that in the event of the servo failing, normal braking action was retained.

Power transmission to the rear wheels was by way of either a double-reduction bevel and spur rear axle, or a worm drive contained within a banjo axle. At speed and on a level road, it was claimed that there was no difference between the axle types, but the double-reduction type was found to be more efficient at low speed and under heavy load, at the cost of a little more noise and a greater need for regular adjustment. As was normal in the period, fuel was lifted from the main tank by way of an Autovac and fed to the carburettor by gravity; an interesting feature fitted was a second delivery pipe from the main tank that was positioned a little lower in the tank and which provided a useful reserve of 2gal (9ltr).

1926 brought the introduction of a forward-control version of the BB chassis, designated FBB, which allowed passenger capacity to be increased to thirty-five and set the traditional body design for the half-cab bus that would remain a common sight on the roads of Great Britain for the next fifty years. Other than relocating the driving position to be alongside the engine, the specifications for the new FBB model remained similar in all respects to the normal-control BB and Premier Six models and was

Lowestoft Corporation purchased two twenty-six seat Guy BB buses fitted with Waveney front-entrance bodies in 1927 and a further three similar vehicles the following year, including fleet number 3 shown here. These were the first motor buses to be operated by the Corporation and were all withdrawn from service by 1940. THE OMNIBUS SOCIETY

INDUSTRIAL RELATIONS IN THE 1920s

On 3 May 1926, a General Strike called by the General Council of the Trades Union Congress commenced in support of coal miners, who had been engaged in a bitter, ongoing dispute with their employers, the pit owners, concerning wage reductions and deteriorating employment conditions. The miners' dispute had its origins in a collapsing market for British-mined coal, both domestically and internationally, due to two prime causes: strong currency rates following the reintroduction of the Gold Standard the previous year, and discounted coal prices forced on Germany as part of the reparation costs from the Great War. With pit owners wishing to retain profitability in a declining market, wages were reduced, layoffs occurred and general conditions of employment worsened.

An earlier strike by the miners had resulted in a lockout by their employers, culminating in the call by the TUC for a General Strike, primarily calling on its members in the railway, transport, printing, docks and iron and steel working industries to support the call. The strike was to last for ten days, with the TUC calling off the action following negotiations with the Government to put into effect the recommendations of a Royal Commission previously set up to investigate the mining industry, and a guarantee from the Government that none of the strikers would be victimized. The guarantee was not forthcoming, so the miners continued to strike, but eventually drifted back to work driven by economic necessity.

In the industrial Midlands, Guy Motors stood out as an employer with an enlightened attitude towards industrial relations and maintaining a good working environment. It is inevitable that disputes would arise from time to time and Guy Motors implemented a forward-looking scheme to ensure that such disputes could be resolved to the satisfaction of both sides without escalation. All employees were required to sign an undertaking that outlined the obligations on both sides of industry should a dispute arise. The undertaking was as follows:

I agree not, under any circumstances, to cease work or go slow until the matter under dispute has been reported in writing within 48 hours' notice by the Works Committee to the General Works Manager who the firm undertake will reply within 48 hours. Failing a satisfactory reply, the matter, in writing shall be referred to the Managing Director within 48 hours' notice, who undertakes to reply within 48 hours. If the reply is unsatisfactory the Committee can refer the matter to the Executive of the Trades Union, who will communicate with the Managing Director and, providing the answer received is not satisfactory, then, and not till then, will I down tools.

The overall effect was to be that during the period that Guy Motors was under independent ownership, strikes were a very rare occurrence.

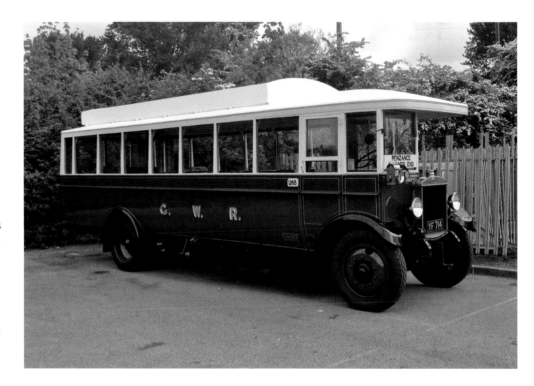

One of the large fleet of FBB buses delivered to the Great Western Railway dating from 1927 and restored to a very high standard, having previously found use as an office building on a caravan site in Cornwall. RICHARD CROCKETT

The drop-frame chassis and pneumatic tyres on this small bus suggest that it is an early BA model. It is seen here in St James' Street in Newport, Isle of Wight, ready to depart on a short journey to Carisbrooke and Gunville ahead of two Southern Vectis vehicles. THE OMNIBUS SOCIETY

usually fitted with the 4-cylinder Guy side-valve engine. A large order for the FBB model was received from the Great Western Railway, fitted with a body of GWR design and constructed by Vickers with a total of thirty-two seats. The seating was arranged in two compartments: twenty-six seats in the forward saloon, and a rear space for smokers fitted with six fold-up seats so that it could also be used for the carriage of parcels.

A new, lightweight chassis, also introduced in 1926, was intended to serve the market for operators who needed to carry between sixteen and twenty passengers and was designated as the Guy ON chassis. Featuring a new 4-cylinder ohv engine rated at 19.2HP, the engine and gearbox design was unusual for Guy in that it featured a bellhousing bolted to both engine and gearbox and containing the clutch, which remained as the cone type.

SIX-WHEEL CHASSIS

In a year noted for the range of new designs to emerge from Guy's Fellings Park facility, perhaps the most notable was to be the BX model introduced to fulfil a requirement for higher capacity buses, driven by continued urbanization of the country and the need for workers to travel to work in the new factories being built outside town centres. To overcome the weight restrictions imposed by the Ministry of Transport, the new range was launched as a six-wheel chassis, comprising the usual two steering wheels at the front and a four-wheel rear bogie, all of which were powered. The prototype model was fitted with a fifty-six seat body by Dodson with an open rear staircase and was placed into service locally in Wolverhampton. It retained the normal-control layout, at a time when there was a general move towards forward control to maximize passenger capacity, and remained in service until 1936, having been rebuilt to the CX model that was to follow.

Early orders followed, with Birmingham Corporation placing an order in 1926 for a BKX, a BX fitted with the 6-cylinder Knight engine and a fifty-eight seat body by Short Brothers. This vehicle, which was to remain in service until 1933, was the first Guy model to be purchased by Birmingham Corporation, which had hitherto been large users of both Daimler and Tilling-Stevens chassis. Although the 1930s would see small numbers of Guys supplied to the city, either on loan for evaluation or outright purchases, it would not be until much further in the future that an order for vehicles of any size would be obtained.

Seen in one of the leafy suburbs of Birmingham on a football special excursion is this Guy BKX fitted with a fifty-eight seat double-deck body built by Short Brothers. This was to be the first Guy bus purchased by the city of Birmingham, which would in the future operate a substantial fleet. AMRTM/GUY ARCHIVE

The same vehicle, seen from the front in the same leafy suburb on a route to the south-west of the city. Abandoned in the middle of what is now a busy junction, this is clearly a posed shot as the driver is missing from the cab. AMRTM/GUY ARCHIVE

Morecambe Corporation Tramways obtained a fleet of six BX models, also bodied by Short Bros, with an open stairway and top deck exposed to the elements providing seating for fifty-three passengers, and powered with the standard Guy 4-cylinder engine. Despite the continued use of an open top, these Morecambe vehicles were forward control, with the half-cab driver's compartment that would rapidly become universal. Although the upper body did not extend above the cab, a full-width canopy was fitted. This fleet, along with the Wolverhampton prototype, were the first double-deck buses to run on pneumatic tyres, an achievement assisted not just by the better distribution of vehicle weight across three axles, but also rapid improvements in tyre technology.

Commercial Motor had for some time in the middle 1920s been a strong proponent for the adoption of six-wheel chassis both for passenger vehicles and goods vehicles, and took great pleasure in promoting the wisdom of its philosophy in an edition published in July 1926, coinciding with the Wolverhampton and Morecambe vehicles entering service, and emphasizing especially the smooth riding of the buses where road irregularities were

'smoothed down in a remarkable manner'. The magazine article mentioned orders in hand for the new chassis at the time of publication: Wolverhampton, seven; Morecambe, six; Oldham, three; Birmingham, one; Norwich Tramways, four; and a single-deck, six-wheel chassis for Salford.

The innovative rear-wheel assembly was of semi-bogie design, meaning that it was able to pivot around a fulcrum mounted across the chassis, but all four wheels remained parallel with the chassis at all times. Although there had been some concern that such a design would increase tyre wear, early reports were that any tyre scrubbing that did occur was limited only to situations where the vehicle was executing a full-lock turn, something that was unusual in normal day-to-day service and, in any case, the reduction in tyre wear from wheel spin, which was now totally eliminated, more than compensated for any scrubbing. The bogie consisted of two axles, both driven and braked, with each side containing a pair of semi-elliptical springs with the ends joined at the axles and the centre points attached to the fulcrum. The usual dropped chassis was raised over the bogie and dropped at the rear to support the

One of the Guy BX vehicles fitted with an open Short Brothers body supplied to Morecombe Corporation showing the adoption of the half-cab, forward-control layout that would quickly become universal.

loading platform and, in common with other Guy chassis designs, the engine and gearbox were mounted in a subframe.

A novel solution was adopted for braking, with each rear hub fitted with brake drums. The forward pair of brakes was operated by the handbrake and the rear set by the foot brake. At the low speeds expected and not much other traffic on the roads, such limited braking power was clearly thought to be adequate, but it has to be said that with both rear axles powered and interconnected by

a common propeller shaft, the effect of braking one axle would automatically retard the other.

A 'feather in the cap' for Guy Motors followed in 1927 when the London Public Omnibus Company (LPOC) obtained permission from the Metropolitan Police to operate a six-wheeled double-deck omnibus in London. LPOC had been formed when a number of independent operators in the central area of London linked up their businesses as a single entity, with plans to replace an existing fleet of around 400 four-wheeled buses with a new

GUY SIX-WHEEL PASSENGER CHASSIS SPECIFICATION

Layout
Normal-control or forward-control six-wheel chassis suitable for single- or double-deck bodywork

Engine
Cylinders — 4-cylinder in-line, of Guy manufacture, or 6-cylinder in-line of Daimler-Knight design
Cooling — Water, traditional radiator, cooling fan driven by engine and circulation by thermo syphon
Bore and stroke — 4-cylinder: bore: 4.25in (107.95mm), stroke: 5.5in (139mm); 6-cylinder: bore: 3.8in (97mm), stroke 5.11in (130mm)
Capacity — 4-cylinder: 5.1ltr; 6-cylinder: 5.76ltr
Valves — 4-cylinder: 2 valves per cylinder; 6-cylinder: 2 sleeves per cylinder

Transmission
Clutch — 4-cylinder: Ferodo friction material faced cone; 6-cylinder: single plate
Gearbox — Four forward speeds and reverse
Overall ratios:
1st — 35:1
2nd — 21.87:1
3rd — 15.1:1
4th — 8.75:1
Reverse — 33.75:1

Suspension and steering
Suspension — Semi-elliptic front, dual semi-elliptic arranged as a semi-bogie to rear
Steering — Marles steering box

Axles
Front — H section
Rear — Fully floating, horizontal banjo casing with worm final drive, both differential units interconnected by a short propeller shaft; final drive ratio 8.75:1

Electrical system — Dynamo and starting motor; ignition by magneto; electric lighting

Brakes
Type — Foot brake operating by rods to drums on rear axle of bogie
Handbrake — Lever operating on front axle of bogie

Dimensions
Track — Both models: 6ft 3in (1,905mm) (front); 6ft 2in (1,880mm) (rear)
Wheelbase — 4-cylinder model: 15ft (4,572mm); 6-cylinder model:15ft 9.5in (4,813mm)
Overall length — 4-cylinder model: 24ft 7in (7,493mm); 6-cylinder model: 25ft 1.75in (7,665mm)

One of the first six-wheeled buses to operate in London, this Dodson-bodied sixty-seat bus built on a Guy BX chassis is seen with a very light load. Of note are the open staircase and the limited weather protection for the driver. NATIONAL MOTOR MUSEUM

fleet of six-wheeled vehicles, both single- and double-decked. The Managing Director of the group had concluded that a fleet of larger capacity buses would help to solve the growing traffic difficulties in the City and West End and, in due course, the authorities at Scotland Yard gave permission for six-wheeled buses running on pneumatic tyres with a seating capacity of sixty-two to be operated. The first service ran in September 1927 between Victoria Station and Winchmore Hill, a route with heavy loadings and close headways, and it was found that its power, braking and general smooth running fully confirmed the objectives set out in the proposal to operate the vehicles.

With a body by Dodson, the original vehicle had seating for sixty passengers: twenty-eight downstairs and thirty-two in the upper saloon. Interesting features of the body were the full-drop windows fitted for ventilation, and the slight extension of the upper saloon forward of the front bulkhead, so that the front row of seats was positioned directly over the bulkhead. London regulations still required the driver to be seated outside, exposed to all the elements, so a normal-control chassis was used with a canopy extending to the front of the vehicle and

the side bodywork extended at waist rail height to the radiator.

B MODELS BECOME C MODELS

In 1927, the B models evolved to be redesignated as C models, an important change being the substitution of the 6-cylinder Daimler Knight sleeve-valve engine to a 6-cylinder ohv motor of Guy design. Both normal- and forward-control models remained available, with forward control rapidly becoming universally adopted for double-deck vehicles and single-deck service buses, while normal control was to remain a popular choice for touring coaches into the 1930s.

One of the more unusual applications of a Guy six-wheel chassis in 1928 was the introduction of sleeper coach services by a business trading as Land Liners Ltd. Two Guy FCX vehicles were fitted with specialist bodies by Strachan & Brown, consisting of accommodation that could be converted to bunks. A toilet was also fitted and catering facilities were provided on the service that ran overnight between London and Manchester.

Lowestoft Corporation continued to purchase Guy vehicles, with a further four single-deck FC models being delivered in 1931. Shown here is fleet number 7, fitted, like the others in the batch, with a thirty-six seat forward-entry bus body built by the local firm of United, which would eventually be absorbed into the well-known firm of Eastern Coach Works, based in the town. Three of the batch were withdrawn in 1946, with number 8 lasting a year longer. THE OMNIBUS SOCIETY

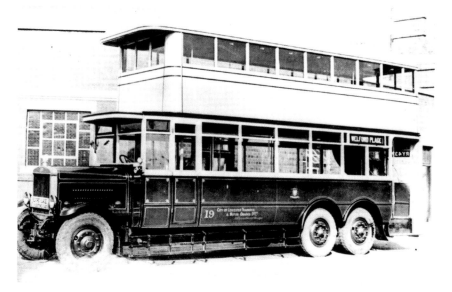

The city of Leicester Tramways Department purchased this single Guy CX with a Brush fifty-six seat body in 1927, followed by a further batch of ten the same year, five the following year, and seven in 1929. Number 19, the original in the fleet, lasted in service until 1939, when it was withdrawn. THE OMNIBUS SOCIETY

C-TYPE MODELS

Model	Wheels	Wheelbase	Decks	Seating Capacity
C	4	16ft 5in (5,004mm)	single	28
FC	4	16ft 5in (5,004mm)	single	32
FC	4	16ft 5in (5,004mm)	double	48
CX	6	16ft 7in (5,055mm)	single	32
CX	6	18ft 6in (5,639mm)	double	66
CX	6	19ft 1.5in (5,830mm)	single	39
CX	6	19ft 1.5in (5,830mm)	double	72

Forward-control versions of CX models were designated with an F prefix to give FCX models with typically an additional two seats on single-deck models and up to six additional seats on double-deck models, depending on body style.

Local to the factory, Wolverhampton Corporation Transport took a number of Guy CX and FCX buses with bodies variously by Dodson, Brush and Guy Motors' own coachwork. Illustrated here, fleet number 64 from 1928 and lasting in service for ten years, has an elegantly styled Dodson fifty-five seat body, with the front now extending slightly over the front canopy. Mazawattee Tea was a popular blend, the owners of which were amongst the first to exploit the benefits of widespread advertising on the sides of buses.
WOLVERHAMPTON CITY ARCHIVE

The Guy-based vehicles operated by Land Liner could accommodate forty-four passengers when operating by day and twenty-one at night, arranged as four four-berth cabins, two two-berth cabins and one single berth. The crew comprised a driver and a steward who rotated their duties every two and a half hours. The vehicle measured 30ft (9,144mm) overall length and 7ft 6in (2,286mm) wide, the maximum dimensions permitted at the time for a six-wheel vehicle, and had an overall height of 13ft 9in (4,191mm) with a weight of just under 8 tons. It was finished in a livery of Mitcham Brown and Citrus Yellow with signwriting showing the destinations on the sides and the fare table on the rear. Day coaches left the terminals at 10am each morning, with the overnight service departing London at 11pm and Manchester at 10:30pm, Monday to Friday. The fare charged was 12s 6d for daytime travel and 15s 6d overnight, and a simple breakfast of rolls, butter and eggs was provided, along with hot drinks, all cooked on a simple Primus stove fitted in the on-board kitchen. Ten hours were allowed to cover the journey of just over 200 miles (320km).

Overnight services from London to the north of England were becoming popular in the late 1920s. In general, reclining seats were fitted, but at the same time as Land Liner started their service, a competitive offering was provided by a firm operating under the name of Al-batross between London and Liverpool, and a planned operation was announced between London and Newcastle. Express Motors had been running a service between Liverpool and Newcastle using Guy coaches fitted with bunks, but these early efforts to provide sleeping accommodation were ahead of their time and most overnight, long-distance services continued to be operated by conventionally seated vehicles, even with the vastly improved road network in the second half of the twentieth century.

SMALL CHASSIS MODEL REVISIONS AT THE END OF THE 1920s

In the same manner that the B models evolved into the C models, enhancements to the smaller ON models transformed this into the OND normal-control and ONDF forward-control model designed for a single-deck bus, or a touring coach body with a capacity of around twenty seats. A key point of this new vehicle was the ability to travel at higher speeds than had previously been possible, with road tests suggesting that 49mph (79km/h) when fully loaded had been achieved. A report in *Commercial Motor* in October 1928 enthusiastically described the new OND under the headline of 'The Fast 20-Seater'.

Although creating the impression that it was a publicly owned undertaking, Cheltenham District Traction Company remained in private hands until the late 1940s. A small number of Guy BB buses were operated, but the fuel filler located on the offside and the familiar 'Feathers in our Cap' radiator cap suggest that this might be a later OND model. It is waiting in Clarence Street in Cheltenham, a location that remains a busy bus interchange point. THE OMNIBUS SOCIETY

Chassis construction utilized ¼in thick steel side members pressed to form a channel section of 6in (152mm) in height with a 2.5in (63.5mm) flange, with the engine and gearbox carried on the traditional Guy three-point mounting subframe and the side rails positioned using a mixture of pressed and tubular cross-members. Semi-elliptic springs provided the suspension, four-wheel braking was fitted and a single-plate clutch connected the engine to the four-speed gearbox. The review placed much emphasis on ease of maintenance, noting inspection covers for the timing gear and starter motor Bendix drive and mentioning the ease of removing the engine and gearbox from the front of the vehicle, in addition to commenting that fitting all the engine ancillaries on the near side made access simple even in a forward-control installation. The maximum weight of the bus was not to exceed 2 tons 5cwt (2,300kg) and the price for the chassis, including lighting, starter and brake servo, was stated to be £445.

A forward-control version of the OND chassis, here in service on the Isle of Wight with Southern Vectis, is waiting for its next service in St James' Square in Newport. THE OMNIBUS SOCIETY

GUY OND PASSENGER CHASSIS SPECIFICATION

Layout	Normal-control or forward-control four chassis suitable for small capacity single-deck bodywork	**Suspension and steering**	
		Suspension	Semi-elliptic front and rear springs
		Steering	Marles steering box
Engine		**Axles**	
Cylinders	4-cylinder in-line, of Guy manufacture, rated at 20HP	Front	H section
Cooling	Water, traditional radiator, cooling fan driven by engine and circulation by thermo syphon	Rear	Fully floating, horizontal banjo casing with worm final drive; final drive ratio 5.4:1
Bore and stroke	Bore: 4-cylinder: 3.5in (90mm), stroke: 5.12in (130mm) stroke	Electrical system	Dynamo and starting motor; ignition by magneto; electric lighting
Capacity	3308cc		
Valves	4-cylinder: 2 valves per cylinder, ohv design by pushrods and rockers	**Brakes**	
		Type	Duplex rear drums with footbrake operating one set of rear shoes and front brake drums, operated through a Dewandre servo
Transmission			
Clutch	Ferodo friction material, single plate	Handbrake	Lever operating on rear wheels, utilizing second part of duplex drums
Gearbox	Four forward speeds and reverse		
Overall ratios:			
1st	28.4:1	**Dimensions**	
2nd	14:1	Track	4ft 9.5in (1,460mm)
3rd	9.2:1	Wheelbase	12ft 3in (3,734mm)
4th	5.4:1	Overall length	18ft 10in (5,740mm)
Reverse	44.4:1		

ACQUISITIONS, MERGERS AND FINANCIAL WORRIES

Mergers and acquisitions in the motor industry were commonplace in the 1920s, as prospering manufacturers took the opportunity to incorporate their less successful rivals, or to acquire technology and gain market share. As the 1920s drew to a close, Guy Motors were to be both target and predator. The Star Engineering Company, another Wolverhampton-based vehicle manufacturer, ran into difficulties in 1927–8 with falling sales, leading to it being absorbed into Guy Motors by way of a share exchange, but with Star continuing to trade under its own name, now legally known as Star Motor Company Limited.

There were two products that may have been of interest to Sydney Guy in undertaking this venture. On the one hand, Star produced a range of expensive, quality cars and it is possible that Guy may have seen this as an opportunity to re-enter the car market. Despite their quality, the cars were too expensive for the market conditions and a loss was being made on every car that was sold. Star were also building small commercial vehicles and a lightweight twenty-seat passenger vehicle, the Star Flyer, a model that was competitive with Guy's own products. Rationalization followed the acquisition, with Star's heavier goods vehicles being discontinued, but it was insufficient to save the company, which was eventually put into receivership in 1932.

Guy Motors rescued the Star Motor Company in 1928. One of the products that would have been of interest to Guy was the Star Flyer, a lightweight chassis designed for small bus bodies, but also suitable for use as a van or small lorry. Production of the Flyer and Star cars continued with a reduced workforce. WOLVERHAMPTON CITY ARCHIVE

Another successful contemporary producer of commercial vehicles whose history closely echoes that of Guy Motors was the firm of Dennis Brothers Ltd, based in Guildford in Surrey. Dennis had earlier purchased the White & Poppe business in 1919, an early supplier of engines to Guy, and by the middle of the 1920s, Dennis and Guy were competitors in the same businesses – both goods vehicles and passenger vehicles. With healthy profits reported for 1927, Dennis made a bid to purchase Guy, a bid that nearly succeeded. With increasing profits, a merger between Dennis and Leyland Motors was also envisaged, but that too did not proceed. Despite the high profit levels, the threat of takeover from Dennis receded in the following years, as the profits of Guy Motors steadily increased. On the sales front, Dennis became less of a competitor in the following years, as the profits were returned to shareholders as dividends while Guy chose to reinvest.

October 1929 saw the Wall Street Crash, with stock values worldwide plummeting. In a panic-driven market, many investors in companies placed orders to sell their stocks at any price, which led to shares in Guy Motors falling to 50 per cent of their previous value. The market continued to decline, with the result that Guy shares eventually reached their lowest point, that of £1 shares now having a value of one shilling (5p), a loss of 95 per cent of their capital value. It was only the goodwill earned through the quality of its products that was to save the company.

THE SIX-WHEEL BUS

The trade magazine *Commercial Motor* had long been a proponent of the six-wheel chassis for use in public transport. In late 1929, a series of features looked at this very subject, concluding that the limit of 9 tons (9,144kg) fully laden for a four-wheel bus was inadequate, and despite the strictest attention to the detail of vehicle design and use of lightweight materials, a strict enforcement of the law would require some operators to remove seats and limit the capacity of their vehicles. At the time, the maximum vehicle weight for a six-wheel or three-axle vehicle was 12 tons (12,192kg), and the magazine, in parallel with supporting the adoption of six-wheeled buses, was supporting with equal measure a campaign to increase the lower limit by half a ton (508kg).

Sydney Guy was, not surprisingly, a firm supporter of the six-wheel design and made the following points in a letter published on 5 November:

Of course, there are two ways of looking at this matter, one being that the weight limit should be increased so as to allow the largest-seating capacity bus to run on four wheels, in which case the present weight limit of nine tons undoubtedly requires to be increased; but is this the proper way to look at the matter? It is an obvious fact, which is supported by all the road authorities, that the heavier the axle weights the more the damage to the road. Further, the most economical vehicle to operate per passenger (providing there be the traffic to justify it) is the largest-capacity vehicle, and surely the logical conclusion will be that this case is best met by increasing the number of axles, and thereby reducing the axle weights, with consequent reduced road wear, at the same time avoiding the necessity of keeping the seating capacity of the vehicle down to a limit which is not always the most economical.

Mr Guy then provided a list of his firm's customers who agreed with his position. He listed the corporations of Derby, Hull, Leicester, Liverpool, Middlesbrough, Northampton, Oldham, Reading, Rotherham, Wolverhampton and the London Public Omnibus Company and concluded that there were very few four-wheeled vehicles on the road at the time that would meet the limit. He concluded by stating: 'After all, there is nothing particularly new about vehicles with more than two axles; both the tram and the train developed this type years ago.'

In the interest of editorial balance, the magazine included remarks from John Thorneycroft and Company Ltd, confirming that, in their opinion, it was not possible to design a suitable two-axle bus within the weight limit without reducing the chassis components to the point where safety was compromised, and also from Messrs Strachans (Acton) Ltd, who blamed chassis builders for excessive weight and said that they were at 'their wits' end' to know where to cut body weight and still be able to guarantee the body to last for four or five years.

As the 1920s came to their close, Guy Motors were in a strong position, notwithstanding the effects of the global financial crisis and fall in the market capitalization value of the business. Their products had gained a reputation for robustness and value that set the company on a strong footing as the 1930s approached.

Chapter 3

GUY TROLLEYBUSES

Horse-drawn and latterly electrically operated tramways had become an established form of transport in many cities worldwide in the late nineteenth and early twentieth centuries. During the 1920s, the advent of the petrol-powered motor bus with its flexibility of operation was beginning to challenge the supremacy of the tram. But in urban environments where the electricity generating concern was often municipally owned, the electric tram had an operational cost advantage. On the other hand, the cost and disruption of track renewals were significant and by the 1920s much of the permanent way was reaching the end of its life, requiring wholesale renewal.

The trolleybus was seen as an interesting development, combining the low cost of electrical propulsion with the comfort of the motor bus. Even running on solid tyres over cobbled roads, the bus and trolleybus could offer a smoother ride than the tramways. The overhead infrastructure was still required, using the same electrical supply as the trams, but the track could be removed and, with increasing road traffic, a safety enhancement was that trolleybuses were able to pull into the kerb in the same manner as motor buses to load and unload passengers.

When extensions were required to routes, supporters of trolleybuses proposed that it was a simple matter to install additional overhead supply, although in reality it was not quite so straightforward, as the electrical supply would need to be augmented, requiring additional generating capacity, new feeder stations and additional switch gear. The wiring for trolleybus systems is inherently more complex than for tramways, because, simply put, trams use the running lines as part of the circuit for the supply of power, whereas trolleybuses running on the road

Guy Motors provided this BTX, fitted with a distinctively styled fifty-three seat body built by Guy, on loan to Birmingham Corporation Transport between 1930 and 1931. Two other Guy vehicles, another BTX and a BT, were loaned for short periods during the same period for testing, but none was purchased. THE OMNIBUS SOCIETY

require a second cable to complete the circuit. Where these cross, it is necessary to provide insulation and complications arise with junctions, where it is essential to ensure that the power-collecting trolley follows the route of the bus if the bus is not to come to an abrupt halt. This all came at a time when the demand for electricity for both industrial and domestic use was increasing. Even then, it was seen as a clean source of power, notwithstanding the heavy pollution caused by the coal-fired generating stations, many of which were located in the middle of urban areas.

Guy Motors were not the first to manufacture a trolleybus, but the company embraced the market wholeheartedly with the introduction of the six-wheel chassis. It will be recalled that Sydney Guy had a thorough grounding in electrical engineering from his apprenticeship years and early employment, so coupling this with the successful chassis designs would clearly lead to commercial success as a builder of trolleybuses.

Close to the Guy Works, Wolverhampton Corporation had been investigating trolleybuses since 1923, when the first of a fleet of thirty-two trolleybuses using a chassis built by Tilling-Stevens and single-deck body by Dodson had been delivered. The chassis was based on the TS6 petrol-electric bus, an interesting design concept developed by Tilling-Stevens at a time when mastering the non-synchromesh crash gearbox of the time was a challenge and the petrol-electric transmission was seen as a solution. Rather than a mechanical drive, this design incorporated an electric motor to drive the vehicle, with the power for the motor obtained from a generator driven by a petrol engine. It is interesting that the world has now come full circle, as this is conceptually what we would recognize, with the addition of high-capacity batteries, as the modern hybrid vehicle.

The difficulty recognized by Wolverhampton Corporation was that the single-deck trolleybus did not provide the passenger capacity that was needed. The solution was to come with the BTX design from Guy, which was based on the recent six-wheel petrol-powered chassis fitted with an electric traction motor. Guy made the decision to fit the traction motor at the front of the vehicle rather than under the floor, allowing a physically larger and therefore more efficient motor to be installed. Electric motor control is substantially different to that of an internal combustion engine, as indeed are the power characteristics. An internal combustion engine develops its maximum torque at a rotational speed usually between 30–70 per cent of its maximum revolutions. For an electric motor, the maximum torque is when the motor is stationary and power is first applied. Internal combustion engines therefore need gears to adjust the engine speed and torque to the desired output.

Electric motors, while they do not require gears, do need some form of controlling system to reduce the starting current and burning out when power is initially applied and this was traditionally provided by using high-power resistors to control the applied current. An electric motor is basically a magnetic machine comprising a rotating coil (the armature) and an external, stationary coil (the field). Field coils then take two forms, either a series coil, connected in series with the armature coil, or a shunt coil, connected in parallel across the armature. In high-power motors, a combination of both series and shunt coils is used. By controlling the current passing through the coils, the output of the motor can be easily controlled and it is therefore seen that more efficient speed control, especially from a standing start, can be gained with a shunt-wound coil, as the current flowing in it can be controlled independently from that flowing in the armature. The various resistors are brought into circuit and the connections between series windings and shunt windings are made through a control box operated electro-mechanically by a speed control, usually operated by the driver's left foot, although Guy would adapt the location of controls to suit the customer's exact requirements.

REGENERATIVE BRAKING – A FIRST FOR GUY

In an internal combustion engine, some degree of engine braking is achieved when power is removed and the engine is being driven by the wheels. In an electric motor, under the same conditions, the motor will become a generator, creating electricity rather than consuming it. Connecting an electrical resistance across this power output will create a braking force, the amount of braking effort being proportional to the resistance across the motor. This is sometimes referred to as rheostatic braking, a rheostat being a form of resistor that can be varied, usually mechanically. Therefore, by judicious design, an electric vehicle can use its motor to provide a form of braking independent of the usual friction braking on the wheels.

In 1926, there was nothing new in rheostatic braking; it was a principle well understood. But what was different, and a new feature introduced by Guy, was a system of regenerative braking. Now, instead of the energy created by braking being dissipated as heat in the rheostats, it was fed back into the supply to augment the power available. Thus, vehicles approaching a stop or travelling downhill were able to return power to the network to be used by other vehicles, thereby reducing the demand on the generating station. This feature was to remain unique to Guy Motors until 1933. Friction brakes were still required to bring the vehicle to a complete halt and a mechanical parking brake was also fitted. Today, regenerative braking is widely used in electric vehicles, with the energy recovered being used to charge the vehicle's batteries.

The first BTX was fitted with a body by Dodson, seating sixty-one passengers – thirty-three in the upper saloon and twenty-eight downstairs. Access to the upper saloon was by a rear open staircase and the body was traditional in the sense that the upper saloon front abutted onto the front bulkhead, with the driver occupying an enclosed cab in front. It became number 33 in Wolverhampton's fleet until 1937, when it was returned to Guy Motors, having covered over half a million miles in daily service and in the expectation of it joining a still-born company museum, before finally being scrapped in 1941. Number 33 was followed in 1927 by an additional seventeen BTX chassis also fitted with Dodson bodies, but now with enclosed staircases and the upper front bulkhead extending partway over the driver's cab. A further six similar models were delivered in 1928, another four in 1929 and a final batch of nine in 1930. Wolverhampton Corporation continued to purchase Guy BTX trolleybuses up until 1932, but the later deliveries were fitted with some bodies of Guy's own manufacture and some that continued to be fitted with the Dodson style. From 1933 onwards, orders were split between Guy Motors and Sunbeam.

Hastings Tramways purchased a mixed fleet of BTX trolleybuses between 1928–9; all were bodied by Ransomes, with the single-deck vehicles seating thirty-two and using a central entrance. The double-deck vehicles with an open rear staircase were supplied with open tops. Although other seaside resorts subsequently converted trolleybuses to open top for seafront services, those supplied to Hastings appear to have been the only trolleybuses supplied from new with open tops. One of the double-deck vehicles has been preserved and is still operational, but with the closure of the trolleybus system the electrical equipment has been removed and replaced with a Commer TS3 two-stroke diesel engine.

Delivered in 1926, Wolverhampton's first double-deck trolleybus on a Guy BTX chassis with a body by Dodson poses outside the depot in Cleveland Road. WOLVERHAMPTON CITY ARCHIVE

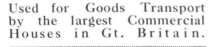
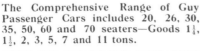

Advertising material by Guy Motors proclaiming themselves as the world pioneer of the six-wheel double-deck trolleybus.

with a 16ft 4.5in (4,991mm) wheelbase to accommodate bodywork of up to 26ft (7,925mm) and sixty passengers over two decks; and BTX66, which would accommodate bodywork, either single- or double-decked, of up to 27ft (8,232mm). In double-deck form, the BTX66 was specified for up to sixty-six passengers. In all the BT range, electrical equipment was originally sourced from Rees-Roturbo, with later models being fitted with equipment supplied by the Electric Construction Company Ltd, whose main factory was located just a few hundred yards from the Guy Motors factory in Fallings Park. ECC Ltd had a proven business in electrical traction equipment as suppliers to tramways and was a significant provider of municipal generating equipment. It continued in business as a provider of high-power electrical equipment until 1985 when the company was finally closed, by which time it had become a part of the Hawker Siddeley combine.

The BT series of trolleybuses was to be successful for Guy Motors; after a gap in production between 1939 and 1947, the final Guy BT was not built until 1950. And it was not just domestic customers that turned to Guy for trolleybuses – the municipal undertakings in both Cape Town and Johannesburg took early deliveries of trolleybuses and remained loyal Guy customers for many years to come, while Japan bought a BT32 single-deck vehicle.

The trolleybus catalogue from Guy consisted of four models, two of which were twin-axle designs given the designation BT32 and intended to be fitted with a single-deck body with seating for up to thirty-five passengers on a wheelbase of 17ft 3.5in (5,270mm). BT48 was the double-deck two-axle chassis intended to accommodate typically fifty-four passengers. In addition, two versions of the BTX six-wheel chassis were also listed: BTX60,

Inside the depot of Hastings Tramways three of the fleet of thirty Ransomes, Simms and Jeffries Ltd bodied single-deck Guy BTX trolleybuses can be seen. Number 50 and number 46, parked behind, are both from the final batch that entered service between 1929–30. HARRY LUFF/ONLINE TRANSPORT ARCHIVE

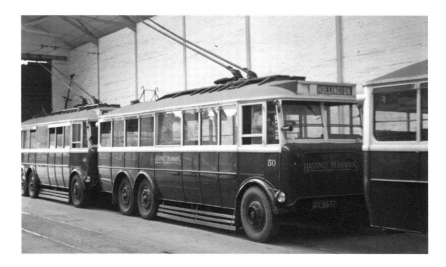

Examples of both types of Guy BTX trolleybuses that were operated in Hastings wait at the junction of Robertson Street and Havelock Road in the town. The buildings in the background survive, but the cinema has become a wine bar. GEOFF WOLFE/1066 ONLINE

The surviving Dodson bodied BTX still running under the wires is seen here outside the 'Bo Peep' public house, just back from the seafront at St Leonards, west along the coast from Hastings. The name of the pub and surrounding area is said to have its origins in the nursery rhyme and is attributed to smugglers who were once active in the area and would return 'wagging their tails [contraband] behind them'. The picture dates from 1953. GEOFF WOLFE/1066 ONLINE

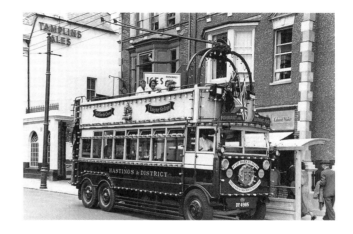

TROLLEYBUS SALES IN THE 1930S

The 1930s were the decade in which the trolleybus really came into its own as tramways reached the end of their lives and were subject to heavy renewal costs. With the electrical infrastructure already in place, conversion to trolleybus operation was seen as advantageous in many Council chambers and various studies showed that electrical operation was more cost-effective than the contemporary petrol-engined motor bus. That would start to change later as buses powered by diesel engines took over from petrol, but through the 1930s Guy became an important supplier to numerous former tramways.

Wolverhampton and Hastings have already been mentioned; South Lancashire Transport closed all but 3 miles (5km) of its tramway system and converted to trolleybus operation in the first three years of the new decade,

using thirty BTX trolleybuses with low-bridge bodies by Charles H. Roe and seating fifty-eight passengers, twenty-nine in each saloon, apart from the initial delivery of ten, which had seating for two more passengers upstairs. These bodies embodied the flat-front style, with a full-width cab and the upper saloon extended fully over the cab, and wore the red and white livery lined out in gold and black, some examples lasting until the closure of the system in 1958. A further batch of fifteen two-axle vehicles followed in 1933, again fitted with Roe low-bridge bodies seating forty-eight passengers, twenty-two downstairs and twenty-six upstairs. These South Lancs vehicles were not fitted with traction batteries and were unable to move off the power, so in situations where it was essential for the vehicles to venture away from the overhead, for example to move around roadworks, an improvised solution using a set of long jump leads was adopted,

The progenitor of the South Lancashire Transport trolleybus fleet, a Guy BTX with Roe low-bridge body, is seen here in unrebuilt form. The positioning of the exterior front lamps extending from the front bodywork is of note. HARRY LUFF/ONLINE TRANSPORT ARCHIVE

Photographed in the same location, number 40 was delivered to South Lancs in 1933 on a four-wheel Guy BT chassis, but by the time this photograph was taken, the front bodywork had been rebuilt in the early 1950s by Bond at Wythenshawe. Although the frontal appearance has changed, the lighting equipment remains mounted externally to the bodywork. HARRY LUFF/ONLINE TRANSPORT ARCHIVE

Number 26, another six-wheel BTX, was delivered in 1931 and withdrawn from service in 1955 in original form. In this image, the bus is turning right into what is thought to be High Street in Atherton, with the conductor, who has presumably just worked the frog in the overhead wiring, chasing after his bus. Following behind is number 69 heading to Bolton, a later Sunbeam MS2 dating from 1948 and fitted with a Weymann body. HARRY LUFF/ONLINE TRANSPORT ARCHIVE

something that would almost certainly not meet with health and safety approval in modern times.

Derby Corporation was another customer purchasing a fleet of seventy-six BTXs that were placed into service between 1932–6. Bodies were provided by a variety of builders, with the bulk coming from Brush and accommodating fifty-six passengers (thirty upstairs; twenty-six in the lower saloon) and others from Dodson and Weymann with broadly similar seating capacities. The last of these remained in service until 1953.

A particularly stylish design was put into service by Newcastle Corporation when it commenced trolley-

bus operations in 1935. In common with some other undertakings, the Corporation employed a multiple vendor policy, with the initial batch of thirty vehicles being split equally between Guy, AEC and Karrier. All shared similar 30ft (9,144mm) long bodywork style, with a conventional open rear platform and folding doors positioned just behind the lower deck front bulkhead for disembarking passengers. The majority of the sixty-seat bodies were built by Metro-Cammell. Newcastle Corporation was to purchase a further three Guy vehicles in 1936, ten in 1937 and a final batch of ten in 1938.

Using the lighting batteries to provide motive power was an innovative solution to allow trolleybuses to be moved when not connected to the overhead power, and was promoted by Guy Motors in this insert to a trade show directory.

Seen outside the Works of Northern Coachbuilders is this 1938 Guy BTX awaiting delivery for the city's transport department. The straight staircase at the rear in the style favoured by Roe is evident from the positioning of the rear windows, and the railings for a forward staircase are visible. As well as an open platform to the rear, a set of doors was provided at the front of the bus to reduce the time spent at bus stops. IMAGE COURTESY OF NEWCASTLE-UPON-TYNE CITY ARCHIVES

Chapter 4

THE 1930s – TROUBLED TIMES AND UTILITY VEHICLES

Within Guy Motors, a subtle change in product marketing occurred early in 1930. Rather than models being designated by letters of the alphabet, a system that was becoming confusing, a new system of model names came into use, with the current C model single-deck chassis now being known as the Guy 'Conquest' and the double-deck equivalent, the Guy 'Invincible'.

Cheltenham District Traction Company purchased a fleet of ten fifty-one seat Invincible buses, fitted with open-top upper decks that went into service around the outlying areas of the town at the beginning of the decade.

These were powered by the Guy 6-cylinder petrol engine through a four-speed gearbox and in all respects were mechanically similar to the FC model, but this purchase appears to be the first occasion on which the new Invincible name was used.

THE FIRST DIESEL BUSES

Until the early 1930s, the petrol engine had been the only viable option for motor buses, but that did not stop both

Delivered to Newcastle in 1930, this is believed to be an official Works image of a Guy FC built just at the point that the model became known as 'Invincible'. The body is by Hall Lewis, the precursor company to Park Royal Vehicles, and still has an open staircase. JAMES TYPE COLLECTION

UK8047 was built originally as a Guy FC with a Hall Lewis body and loaned to Birmingham Corporation. It was fitted experimentally with a Gardner 5LW diesel engine prior to returning to Guy's Works, where it was rebuilt as an Arab, fitted with a 6LW engine, a Metro-Cammell body and returned to Birmingham with the new registration OC8208.
THE OMNIBUS SOCIETY

suppliers and operators from considering the opportunities that the compression ignition engine would offer. Now universally known as the diesel engine, compression ignition engines had been employed in large stationary installations and as primary motive power for ships since the early years of the century, but were both heavy in relation to their power output and required elaborate procedures to coax them into life, with many requiring a hot plug in the cylinder head to be first heated with a blow lamp to help with initial firings. Furthermore, rather than varying the amount of fuel injected to control the power developed, early engines, intended to run at a near constant speed, were regulated by a 'hit or miss' form of regulation, whereby firing strokes would be omitted entirely to adjust the running speed. It was the introduction of the lightweight and high-speed diesel engine by the likes of Gardner that made the application

of the oil-burning compression ignition a possibility for road transport.

The first recorded experimental installation of a diesel engine in a motor bus was undertaken by the Midlands firm of Barton, which would in the future operate a fleet of Guy vehicles. Originally established in 1897 by Thomas Barton, the business bearing his name would become well known for innovative and distinctive bodywork designs. It was unusual at the time for commercial vehicle operators to consider designs other than from domestic suppliers, but Barton had been impressed by the products offered by the Italian business of Lancia, from whom a number of commercial vehicle chassis were purchased, modified and used as the basis of a fleet of vehicles known as 'Barton Gliders'.

Earlier in his career, Thomas Barton had worked for the Lincolnshire-based firm of Richard Hornsby & Sons, where he had been involved in the development of pioneering heavy oil engines and therefore had an interest in compression ignition engines and the advantages that they might potentially offer. An approach was therefore made to L. Gardner & Sons Ltd of Patricroft in Manchester to supply a marine diesel engine for experimental use in a bus. Although reluctant to become involved, Gardner sold Barton a 4L2 engine that was installed into a Lancia-Barton chassis and put into service in March 1930. This experimental bus proved the viability of compression ignition diesel engines in road transport and especially for buses. It did not go unnoticed by either the bus industry or by Gardner, who later introduced a new model based on the L2 range specifically intended for road transport, designated the LW range, available as a 4-, 5- or 6-cylinder engine.

Following the Barton experiments, Guy offered a diesel engine as an option for the Invincible, creating a relationship that would remain until the end of double-deck bus production by Guy long into the future, although it would be some years before the use of diesel power became universal and there was to be a further model change to come in the story.

An announcement was made in late 1931 introducing the new 1932 model of Conquest and Invincible bus chassis. Apart from the most obvious addition of the option to deliver the chassis fitted with a Gardner diesel engine, a further change was made to the front axle, which now incorporated directly acting vacuum cylinders connected

Dating from around 1930, this advertising feature promotes both the Invincible double-decker and the Conquest single-decker. The Invincible appears to be remarkably similar to UK8047.

to the brake assemblies rather than relying on rods. Flexible pipes connected the front cylinders to the master valve located on the main servo, which operated the rear brakes via rods. As was usual practice with Guys, the engine was flexibly mounted in a subframe, with the gearbox mounted further back in the frames than had been usual in earlier models. Power came from a 6-cylinder Gardner 6LW engine governed to 1,650rpm, producing slightly in excess of 100bhp and a maximum torque of 350lb ft at 1,000rpm.

THE 1930 ROAD TRAFFIC ACT

On entering any public service vehicle, the passenger will find a notice that his or her conduct and that of the crew is governed by the Road Traffic Act of 1930. This, coupled with changes to the construction and use

regulations applicable to all vehicles, but especially to heavy vehicles, would have far-reaching effects on Guy Motors and all other manufacturers. The most significant change to public service vehicles instituted a system of regulation and licensing undertaken by newly appointed traffic commissioners, rather than by local authorities, except in the Metropolitan Police district of London, which retained its existing powers. The length of time that a driver could work without taking a break, the requirement to take a daily rest and a limit on the number of hours that could be worked in a single day were also prescribed. On the road in general, the speed limit for cars was abolished, on the grounds that the inability properly to enforce the limits then prevailing brought the entire legal system into disrepute, but a limit for all vehicles in built-up areas of 30mph (48km/h) was normal. This was also the maximum speed for all public service vehicles running on pneumatic tyres. Goods vehicles with an unladen weight of under 2.5 tons (2,540kg) were also restricted to 30mph (48km/h), but heavier lorries were restricted to 20mph (32km/h).

The 1930 Act also paved the way for the introduction of unified Construction and Use Regulations for the United Kingdom, which came into effect in January 1931 and, amongst other changes, increased the maximum permissible weight on dual-axle chassis to the extent that the requirement for six-wheeled vehicles was diminished.

An Unfortunate Effect of the Road Traffic Act

Within the powers of the Road Traffic Act, an order was made restricting the use of one-man operated buses to no more than twenty seats, unless a minimum fare of sixpence (2.5p) was charged, in which case up to twenty-six seats could be accommodated. The market for medium capacity single-deck buses for one-man operation was affected dramatically. *Commercial Motor* noted in April 1932 that the market had changed from 160 new 26 seat vehicles being registered in May 1931, to only four of the type being registered in January 1932.

Birmingham Corporation was using a fleet of thirty normal-control 6-cylinder petrol-engined Guy Conquest buses fitted with twenty-five seat bodies on suburban services, operated by a one-man crew; exactly

SUMMARY OF THE CONSTRUCTION AND USE REGULATIONS

Maximum length	
Four-wheel vehicle	27ft 6in (8,382mm); double-deck buses restricted to 26ft (7,925mm)
More than four wheels	30ft (9,144mm)
Maximum width	7ft 6in (2,286mm)
Maximum overhang	7/24ths of length
Maximum weight (unladen)	
Four-wheel vehicle	7.25 tons
Six-wheel vehicle	10 tons
Maximum weights and axle loading	
Four-wheel vehicle	Axle load: 8 tons
	Maximum laden weight: 12 tons
Six-wheel vehicle	Axle load 7.5 tons
	Maximum laden weight: 19 tons
Glazing	All forward-facing windows, except the upper front windows of a double-deck bus, must be safety glass
Tyres	Vehicles registered after 1 January 1933 must be fitted with pneumatic tyres if used after 1 January 1940

the type of operation that would be prohibited under the new Order. These had been delivered in late 1929 and early 1930, so were generally less than two years old when the Regulations changed. As it would be necessary to employ a conductor, the decision was made to rebuild the buses to a forward-control type with increased capacity, and a quotation for the work was obtained from Guy.

The buses were returned to Fallings Park in batches of five: the bodies were removed; all the mechanical elements were overhauled; and the chassis extended from the original 26ft (7,925mm) to 27ft 6in (8,382mm). A

Number 68 was one of the thirty Guy Conquest buses supplied with Guy bodies, seating twenty-five passengers for 'pay as you enter' operation in Birmingham between 1929–30, that were affected by the changes brought in with the Road Traffic Act. THE OMNIBUS SOCIETY

The Birmingham Conquests were rebuilt between 1931–2, but were to have a short life, with most being withdrawn after just six years. THE OMNIBUS SOCIETY

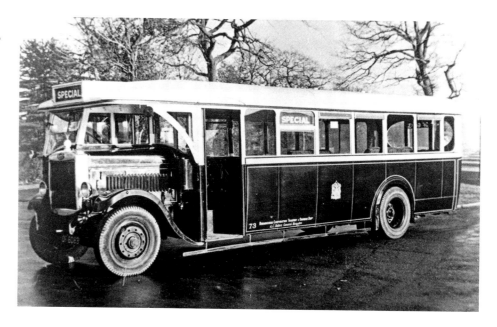

new forward-control cab was constructed and the controls refitted in the same layout as a newly built forward-control Conquest, and an additional section of bodywork fitted. The canopy extended over the bonnet, with a large triangular bracket adding to the rigidity of the roof. The resulting vehicles now seated thirty-two passengers. It was reported that the cost amounted to little more than a complete overhaul, and the entire project was completed within three months.

A NEW COMPETITOR ARRIVES

In 1931, a new competitor entered the market. General Motors of the US had purchased the Vauxhall car business in 1925 and introduced a range of light commercial vehicles under the Bedford brand. Initially, this only threatened Guy's lighter truck business, but in 1935 the WTB bus chassis powered by a 6-cylinder petrol engine originally built for GM's US Chevrolet brand appeared on the scene. With only minor changes, this engine would remain in production into the late 1960s. Just prior to the outbreak of World War II, Bedford launched the model OB bus and coach chassis in conjunction with Duple, who provided a revised version of the bodywork fitted to the WTB, known as the Vista. Once production recommenced following the hostilities, the Duple-bodied OB was to provide stiff competition to Guy's smaller PSV range, becoming the archetype small coach during the early 1950s.

GUY ARAB – A THOROUGHBRED AMONGST BUSES

In the early part of 1933 Guy Motors announced a new product that was to establish firmly the reputation of the company as a manufacturer of bus and coach chassis for the next twenty-five years. Named as the Guy Arab, it also had the distinction of being the first bus chassis to be designed specifically to incorporate a diesel engine. The new Arab model range was supplied suitable for both single-deck and double-deck coachwork; both were available in 26ft (7,925mm) body lengths, with a 27ft 6in (8,382mm) length available for the single-deck version and an export only, six-wheel double-deck version was also listed.

Single-deck versions were designated as FD32 or FD35, depending on length, with the number in the designation giving the notional seating capacity of the body. For the single deck, power was provided by a Gardner 4LW or optionally a 5LW oil engine, while the double-decker, designated FD48, seated up to fifty-six passengers, with power from a 5LW or optionally a 6LW. The export model was coded FDX60.

Many of the details followed the established Guy practice, with the four-speed crash gearbox mounted partway along the chassis. An unusual feature concerned the location of the rear axle pot, this being located on the offside of the vehicle, rather than the more usual near-side. It was said that this feature helped to offset the leaning effect that occurred in city streets with a severe camber by moving some of the weight towards the crown of the road, but, more importantly, when a low-bridge body was fitted with an offset upstairs gangway, it assisted with balancing the loading to the nearside of the bus. To help

in reducing loads in the transmission path, the engine was mounted with a slight offset. Whether the relocation of the axle pot was beneficial is open to question, as it was a feature that was not continued in later versions of the Arab models. The rear brakes incorporated a novel feature whereby each brake drum was acted on by four brake shoes rather than the usual two. All four shoes were

GUY ARAB FD PASSENGER CHASSIS SPECIFICATION

Layout	Forward-control four-wheel or six-wheel (export only) chassis suitable for single- or double-deck bodywork	**Electrical system**	12V electrical system; axial style starter; dynamo; battery capacity 173AH
Engine	Single-deck chassis: Gardner 4LW or 5LW	**Brakes**	
	Double-deck chassis: Gardner 5LW or 6LW	Type	Foot brake operating drums on all wheels; rear drums each fitted with four shoe assemblies
Cylinders	4, 5 or 6 cylinders as suggested by engine model name		to minimize drum distortion; assisted by Dewandre vacuum
Cooling	Water, traditional radiator, cooling fan driven by engine		servo, mounted under driver's seat and supplied by vacuum reservoir
Bore and stroke	Bore: 4.25in (107.95mm), stroke: 6in (152.4mm)		tank of 2,180cu in (35.72ltr); vacuum created by engine-
Capacity	4-cylinder: 5.6 litres		mounted exhauster
	5-cylinder: 7 litres		Front drums 17in diameter × 3in
	6-cylinder: 8.4 litres		wide (432 × 76.2mm)
Valves	2 valves per cylinder		Rear drums 16⅝ diameter × 4⅝in wide (422 × 117.5mm)
Transmission		Handbrake	Push-on lever, operating on all
Clutch	Single-plate friction material		wheels
Gearbox	Four forward speeds and reverse		
Overall ratios:		**Dimensions (FD48 model)**	
1st	20.3:1	Track	Front 6ft 5.25in (1,962mm); rear
2nd	10.9:1		5ft 10in (1,778mm)
3rd	7.6:1	Wheelbase	16ft 7.5in (5,067mm)
4th	4.8:1	Overall dimensions	Length 25ft 7in (7,798mm); width
Reverse	19.5:1		7ft 6in (2,286mm); chassis side members 11in (280mm) in depth at deepest point
Suspension and steering			
Suspension	Semi-elliptic front and rear	Wheels and tyres	Pressed-steel disc type, 20in
Steering	Marles steering box		diameter × 9.75in (front) and 9in (dual rear)
Axles		Fuel tank capacity	35gal (159ltr)
Front	H section	Maximum speed	38mph (61km/h) at engine
Rear	Final drive ratio 4.8:1; final drive offset to offside		governed speed of 1,700rpm

operated simultaneously and had the effect of reducing the tendency of the brake drums to become oval.

An early customer for the new Arab was Blackpool Corporation, which purchased two examples in 1933 with bodies by Brush. An unusual feature of these two vehicles was the centre entrance and staircase. Other early deliveries were to Burton-upon-Trent; the first two delivered in 1934 were a unique normal-control design with bodies seating twenty-six passengers and were most likely the very last normal-control heavyweight chassis buses to be built for the domestic market. A fleet of ten forward-control single-deck Arabs, again with Brush bodies, was supplied in 1935, with further deliveries every year until 1941, when the fleet numbered a total of thirty-one vehicles with seating capacities of between thirty-two and thirty-four. All were powered by the Gardner 4LW engine. Burton-upon-Trent Corporation at this time was running an almost exclusively Guy fleet with just a handful of other chassis and was to continue to prefer Guy vehicles until 1962, when it changed allegiance to Daimler. A large number of low railway bridges in the area around the brewery town restricted the use of double-deck vehicles.

FA5447, the first Guy Arab to be delivered to Burton-upon-Trent Corporation, was fitted with a Brush twenty-six seat body. The large bonnet made for a very distinctive appearance. THE OMNIBUS SOCIETY

FA5856 was numerically the last of a batch of ten Arabs delivered to Burton in 1935 and was again fitted with a Brush body, but now being a forward-control vehicle, seating capacity was increased to thirty-two. THE OMNIBUS SOCIETY

A rear view of the normal-control bodies as fitted to FA5447. The oil lamps for the front side lamps and the rear marker lamp are unusual fittings.
THE OMNIBUS SOCIETY

In the immediate vicinity of the Guy factory, only a handful of the early Arabs were in service. One with an interesting history had started life as a Guy Invincible demonstrator in 1929, fitted with a Hall Lewis body seating forty-eight passengers. Delivered to Birmingham Corporation Transport on extended loan at the very end of 1929, it ran in service for the Corporation as its number 97 and during the loan was fitted with a Gardner 5LW engine. At the end of 1933, it was returned to Fallings Park, where it was rebuilt to exit the Works as a Guy Arab 6LW in 1934 and returned to Birmingham, having acquired a new chassis number and a new Metro-Cammell fifty-one seat body. To confuse matters further, on its return it was given the fleet number 208, this number having been transferred from an older Guy BKX bus that had recently been withdrawn. An image of this vehicle in its original form can be seen towards the beginning of this chapter. In Wolverhampton, the Corporation, having invested heavily in trolleybuses, only purchased limited numbers of motor buses during the 1930s, which included two Arabs in 1935 with Park Royal thirty-two seat single-deck bodies, and a solitary double-decker in 1936 with a Brush fifty-three seat body.

On the south coast, Southampton Corporation Transport had purchased a fleet of twenty single-deck Guy buses, with the first arriving in 1926 and fitted with bodies built in the Corporation's own workshops. Although the Corporation had purchased a small fleet of open-topped double-deckers from Thorneycroft in 1919, these were mostly rebodied with single-deck bodies within four years of delivery. Thereafter, a policy of small capacity motor buses built on chassis supplied by Leyland and Guy dominated the roads of the port town, operating in conjunction with an extensive tramway system. 1929 saw the return to double-deck purchases, with five Thorneycroft vehicles delivered fitted with fifty-six seat English Electric bodies. Three AEC Regent vehicles followed in 1930, with a further ten Thorneycrofts being supplied up to 1934. These were fitted with a variety of bodies, with the fifty-six seat Park Royal being dominant.

It should be noted that Thorneycroft were a Hampshire-based business and had extensive operations in Southampton, which, in the early 1930s – a period plagued by mass unemployment – may have been a consideration, with the Corporation wishing to encourage and support local business. In 1934, two Guy Arabs with fifty-six seat bodies by Park Royal joined the fleet, setting a pattern that was to define the typical Southampton bus for many years in the future. A further eight were delivered in the following year, joined in 1936 by one further Arab and a former Guy Invincible demonstrator fitted with a Strachan body. The Arabs gave good service, lasting until 1950.

Photographed after the Defence Regulations came into effect, as shown by the masked headlamps and white markings to the mudguards, JW8112 was the solitary double-deck pre-war Guy Arab to join the fleet at Wolverhampton, where it was numbered 312. The body by Brush seated fifty-three.
WOLVERHAMPTON CITY ARCHIVE

One of the Southampton buses was displayed at the 1935 Commercial Motor Show, fitted with a new preselective gearbox using a system developed by the French Cotal company, but with adaptations patented by Guy to suit the requirements of a bus operating a frequent start/stop schedule in busy city streets. The basis of this system was an epicyclic gearbox in the same manner as the familiar Wilson preselect system, but rather than using brake bands as in the Wilson system, the Cotal device used electromagnetic clutches to actuate the gear selection. In place of a mechanical gear lever, the driver was provided with an electrical gear selector on a quadrant fitted to the steering column. Gears could be selected in advance, but the gear change, in common with most other preselective systems, did not occur until the driver pressed a pedal fitted in the same location as the conventional clutch pedal. Here was the subtle difference in the Guy implementation, because the native Cotal system operated without the 'clutch' pedal, with gears being selected solely by the movement of the quadrant lever.

An article in *Commercial Motor* in November 1935 describing the system reported that the drive was taken up 'very sweetly' and the system subject to the 'minimum

of wear'. To help the driver know which gear was in use, an illuminated indicator was fitted to the dashboard. Despite the advantages of smoothness of ride and reduction of workload on the driver, the system did not prove to be popular, and few vehicles were fitted with this implementation of preselective control. We shall need to wait until later in the development of the Arab chassis to see the more widespread adaptation of preselect systems, when the Wilson epicyclic gearbox and fluid flywheel would dominate.

Although the economic situation of the country was slowly improving as the 1930s progressed, the world political situation was taking a serious turn, with many believing war with Germany to be inevitable. In such circumstances, it was not surprising that investments in public transport were limited, resulting in lower than anticipated shipments of the early Guy Arab models, something in the order of just sixty vehicles being supplied between its introduction and the end of production in 1939. War, of course, did come at the end of the decade and with Guy Motors being one of only two permitted suppliers of double-deck buses, the other being Daimler, the Arab model was to be given new prominence.

SMALLER VEHICLES OF THE 1930s

Encouraged by the changes implemented in the Road Traffic Act allowing lorries with a laden weight below 2.5 tonnes to travel at a maximum speed of 30mph (48km/h), in 1933 Guy introduced a range of small

Chassis Price, £495

EVERY good quality of a high-class private car is built into this 20-seater coach. A six-cylinder engine of remarkable power and acceleration, with smoothness at all speeds. Springing and seating, safety braking, road-holding and cornering qualities. The most attractive coach on the market, selling extensively throughout the country. Write for demonstration.

GUY

GUY MOTORS LTD., WOLVERHAMPTON

goods vehicles that utilized lightweight materials and construction methods, with the intention also of reducing running costs. Historically, the unladen weight of a lorry had been broadly similar to the maximum load that it could carry, but Guy's new range resulted in an unladen weight far lower than the load capacity. The advantages here were carried forward into a new range of smaller passenger-carrying vehicles that share the names of the lorries: Wolf and Vixen.

Initially, the Wolf CF14 and CF20 models, which were suitable for normal-control bodywork and seated fourteen and twenty passengers respectively, were introduced, followed in 1934 by two larger models, the Vixen 24 and Vixen 26, again suitable for bodies seating nominally twenty-four or twenty-six passengers. The Vixen was suitable for forward-control and half-cab bodies in the traditional style, but was sometimes fitted with a streamlined effect flat full-front body in advance of that type of styling generally coming into fashion some twenty years into the future. All models found ready markets at home and overseas, with examples being shipped to India and Australia.

All were powered by 4-cylinder petrol engines supplied by Meadows, whose business was located adjacent to the Guy Works in Wolverhampton. Braking was mechanical, with a Lockheed hydraulic system being an option. Production ceased in 1939, not recommencing again until 1946.

ABOVE LEFT: The quality of a high-class private car could be experienced in the 1931 Guy Victory twenty seat coach, according to this advertisement. The market for vehicles of this size was about to become very competitive with the introduction of the small Bedford models, a marque that would soon dominate the market for coaches seating between twenty and thirty passengers.

LEFT: Llandudno Borough Council operated a tourist service around the landmark of the Great Orme, purchasing a Guy Wolf with a Roberts semi-open body seating nineteen in 1935 to supplement the existing fleet of Dennis and a single Guy OND vehicle. Prior to restoration, this particular vehicle found service as an ice-cream van. CW

Illustrated above is one of the GUY "VIXEN" 38 seater, 17' 6" wheelbase buses recently supplied to the East India Tramways Co. Ltd. Karachi, who operate a large fleet of GUY buses. For full details and specifications of GUY vehicles suitable for overseas transport, write to:

GUY MOTORS LTD. WOLVERHAMPTON

ABOVE LEFT: Another Wolf followed to Llandudno in 1938, this one fitted with a twenty-seat coach body by Waveney.

ABOVE RIGHT: The Vixen was popular with smaller bus operators and in export markets. Guy Motors shipped twenty-one forward-control Vixens to Karachi, boasting of the achievement with this advertisement. Protection for the driver was minimal.

INTO THE 1940s – THE ARAB UTILITY BUS

In the latter years of the 1930s, Guy Motors found themselves involved in the area of military equipment, developing a new system of welding armoured plate that was to prove beneficial in the coming years. With the outbreak of war in September 1939, the attention of all manufacturing companies, including Guy, was turned to supporting the war effort, with passenger transport severely controlled. All manufacturing of non-essential war effort material was stopped, with partly finished vehicles being stored, or, to quote the Ministry of Supply, 'frozen', initially for the duration of the hostilities. Bus operators were now

GAL224, a Guy Arab I, was delivered to Barton in January 1943 with a low-bridge body by Brush and is seen here in what appears to be as-built form, with a single opening window each side on both decks. The paintwork has some gloss to it, suggesting the photograph originates from after the end of the war. The bus was one of the Arab Is not to be rebuilt. THE OMNIBUS SOCIETY

facing difficulties on numerous fronts. On the one hand, the number of passengers being carried, particularly to the munitions factories, increased dramatically, but on the other, vehicles which had become life-expired could be neither replaced nor overhauled due to non-availability of materials for what was considered to be unessential work. To make matters even worse, the skilled workforce required to continue the maintenance of the vehicle fleet to the high standards required were either being called up for military service, or had been diverted into the construction of war equipment.

The situation was not helped by air raids that seriously damaged or destroyed the existing fleet. Common sense eventually was to prevail, and in 1941, Guy Motors, who at the time had some limited spare capacity following cancelled orders as a result of revisions to the

'TRANSPORT THROUGH THE SYZYGIES' – AN EDUCATION THROUGH ADVERTISING

Advertising during the war years was severely restricted, with a requirement where commercial advertising was permitted that it should have an educational aspect. Guy Motors, anxious to keep the public aware of the company name, its products and contribution to the war effort, embarked on an interesting series of newspaper adverts under the title of 'Transport through the Syzygies'. Each advert carried an image of a current Guy product and its historical equivalent; an armoured car and a Roman chariot in one case and a horse-drawn carriage and Guy Arab bus in another. The word 'Syzygies' caused much puzzlement, with letters to the editors of the newspapers in which the advertising appeared questioning whether there was a spelling mistake, and other letters directly to Guy Motors seeking explanations. All eventually became clear with the publication of a small brochure by the Company containing copies of the original advertisements entitled *Transport Through the Syzygies – An Explanation*, with the first page listing three dictionary definitions of 'Syzygy', which was revealed as being an astronomical term related to the linear arrangement of three celestial bodies. An alternative dictionary definition suggests a further meaning of 'any two related things, either alike or opposite'.

The 'Syzygies' advertising campaign was finally explained in a booklet published by Guy Motors.

defence strategy at the time, were tasked by the Ministry of War Transport, having consulted with the Technical Committee of Operators, to develop a chassis suitable for a low cost and simple double-deck bus. A completed specification was agreed in September of that year and a prototype was available for inspection in early 1942, the intention being that production when it went ahead would be shared between Guy and Leyland. As it transpired, Leyland were heavily committed to building military vehicles and overcoming numerous technical issues with the construction of tanks to the extent that the construction of bus chassis was, initially, undertaken uniquely by Guy Motors.

The basis of the design was the earlier 'Arab', but in the interests of saving essential materials for the war effort, all aluminium items were replaced with cast iron, the most obvious of which was the exposed radiator. Power came from the Gardner LW oil engine, with the majority of the first build of around 500 chassis being fitted with 5-cylinder engines; where the operating terrain was particularly hilly around 15 per cent were fitted with the 6LW. Installation of the larger engine created a key feature of the Arab, in that the extra length of the engine necessitated the radiator being moved further forwards, significantly ahead of the line of the cab, with the front wings being given an outward sweep to meet the line of the radiator. These early build utility buses were designated as Guy Arab Mark 1, usually written as 'Arab I'. Subsequent builds, given the nomenclature, inevitably, of Guy Arab Mark 2, 'Arab II', incorporated the lengthened bonnet and revised front wings even when fitted with the 5LW engine.

With an increase in weight of 18.5 per cent and no additional power being available, the gearing was revised accordingly, manual gearboxes only being permitted, and a double-plate clutch used. The unusual location of the rear axle pot on the offside as fitted to the original pre-war Arab was discontinued, but Guy's preference for the location of the gearbox partway along the chassis was retained, as was the slightly unconventional gear change that resulted in the lower two gears being close to the driver's leg, with third and top gear being in a plane, requiring the lever to be moved to the left, often referred to at the time as a 'Chinese' gearbox. Braking was hydraulic using Lockheed components, assisted by a Dewandre vacuum servo.

To accommodate the additional length of the 6-cylinder Gardner engine, the radiator was positioned further forward in the Arab chassis. For simplicity, all Arab II chassis had the extended bonnet, irrespective of which engine was fitted.

Swindon number 51 is an Arab II with an original Weymann body, supplied to Swindon Corporation in July 1943. When withdrawn it was selected to be preserved for the nation and is now kept in storage by the Science Museum. It is said to be in a fragile condition and is rarely seen. CW

HGC130 is one of the Park Royal-bodied vehicles supplied to London Transport at the end of the war and one that has survived into preservation, now forming part of the London Bus Museum collection at Brooklands. CW

Another bus in the Barton fleet, GNN710, has a low-bridge body by Strachan. CW

Looking neglected and having donated its Gardner 5LW engine, GAL391, another in the Barton fleet new in June 1943, has a low-bridge Duple body that appears to have been modified with rubber-mounted sliding windows. The vehicle parked behind shows how low these bodies were. cw

GUY ARAB I UTILITY PASSENGER CHASSIS SPECIFICATION

Layout	Forward-control four-wheel chassis for double-deck utility bodywork	**Electrical system**	24V electrical system; 38A dynamo with compensated voltage control; 185AH batteries (4 × 6V)
Engine	Gardner 5LW or 6LW by special dispensation	**Brakes**	
Bore and stroke	Bore: 4.25in (107.95mm), stroke: 6in (152.4mm)	Type	Foot brake operating drums on all wheels; hydraulically operated with vacuum servo assistance
Capacity	5-cylinder: 7 litres		Front drums 17in diameter × 3.5in wide (432 × 89mm)
	6-cylinder: 8.4 litres		Rear drums 16.25in diameter × 6.5in wide (412.75 × 165mm)
Valves	2 valves per cylinder	Handbrake	Conventional lever, operating on rear wheels only
Transmission			
Clutch	Dual plate friction material		
Gearbox	Four forward speeds and reverse	**Dimensions**	
Overall ratios:		**(5LW equipped model)**	
1st	1:4.6	Track	Front 6ft 5.25in (1,962mm), rear 5ft 10in (1,778mm)
2nd	1:2.86		
3rd	1:1.7	Wheelbase	16ft 3in (4,953mm)
4th	1:1	Overall dimensions	Length 26ft (7,925mm), width 7ft 6in (2,286mm), chassis side members 11in (280mm) in depth at deepest point
Reverse	1:4.4		
Suspension and steering			
Suspension	Semi-elliptic front and rear		
Steering	Marles steering box	Wheels and tyres	Pressed-steel disc type, 20in diameter × 10.5in (front) and 9in (dual rear)
Axles			
Front	H section		
Rear	Two final-drive ratios were offered, depending on operating conditions: 6.25:1 or 5.6:1	Fuel tank capacity	28gal (113ltr)
		Maximum speed	Determined by rear axle ratio

The service manual for the Guy Arab provided a good schematic view of the chassis, showing the central location of the gearbox, the batteries, fuel tank and brake servo vacuum tank.

Bodywork for the utility vehicles was plain and simple. With shortages of materials, timber framing utilized locally grown, mostly unseasoned softwood with thin steel sheeting replacing the more suitable aluminium, which was more urgently required for aircraft construction. Opening windows were restricted, usually to one each side of each deck, seating was of the wooden slatted type more usually seen in trams, and complex curves in the bodywork were wherever possible completely eliminated. Although built to the same general style, various builders constructed the utility bodies with both low-bridge and high-bridge body styles being supplied, the low bridge generally accommodating twenty-eight passengers in the lower saloon and twenty-seven upstairs, while the high bridge could accommodate fifty-six in total, with thirty sitting upstairs. The regulations on standing passengers were relaxed during peak periods to allow for crush loads, but peak periods were poorly, if at all, defined.

During the design period of the early utility vehicles, the Ministry of Supply sanctioned the use of part-built bodies and components that were in stock at the time,

Reducing the need for skilled labour and scarce materials, utility bus passengers were provided with wooden slatted seats, and in some bodies, the rear emergency exit was left unglazed.

In place of the rear dome, utility bodies used a far simpler construction that eliminated all complex curves.

Looking into the driver's cab of a utility Arab shows that little changed over the years, but at least the driver was treated to a padded seat. The trafficator switch and fire extinguisher are more recent additions.

resulting in a small number of vehicles receiving less austere bodies. It had been said that the Ministry of Supply had 'frozen' production of these unfinished vehicles and therefore, once permission had been granted for them to be completed, they were known as 'unfrozen' buses.

Despite the efforts of Guy to supply the requirements for buses, it was clear that a second chassis builder was required, at which time the Ministry of Supply sanctioned the Daimler Company to recommence construction. Daimler's factory in Coventry had been destroyed during the heavy bombing raids on that city and therefore a replacement would be required before production could recommence. The Ministry of Supply requisitioned suitable premises for Daimler in Wolverhampton, resulting in all double-deck chassis being built in the city. With

Guy trolleybus construction continuing in the war years and the only alternative suppliers being Sunbeam and Karrier, both part of the Rootes Brothers empire and also based in Wolverhampton, all large-capacity passenger transport chassis construction was now located in a small area of the West Midlands. Small capacity single-deck requirements were met by Bedford, with their OWB petrol-engined chassis fitted with an even more austere example of a utility body.

By the time peace came again to Europe, more than 2,000 Guy Arab utility buses had been built, with production of the utility chassis continuing into 1947, by

BODYBUILDERS FOR GUY ARAB I UTILITY BUSES

Coachbuilder	Bodies Built	Comments
Brush	77	
Duple	27	
Massey	45	All high-bridge bodies
Northern Counties	53	All low-bridge bodies
Pickering	18	All high-bridge bodies
Park Royal	106	All high-bridge bodies
Charles H. Roe	56	One high-bridge, remainder low-bridge bodies
Strachan	43	All low-bridge bodies
Weymann	75	All high-bridge bodies
Weymann, completed by Liverpool Corporation	13	

The only single-deck bus available during World War II years was the utility bodied Bedford OWB that featured a most austere body, in this case built by Duple. Although not expected to have a long life, several of the vehicles provided to Portsmouth Corporation remained in service into the 1960s and this example has survived into preservation. The front turn signals are a much later addition; originally the driver may simply have indicated by waving a hand from the front sliding window.

Guy Motors produced a sales catalogue to promote the Arab. Although the body follows the utility style, it is thought that the material was produced after 1945 as it is unlikely that colour printing would have been permitted during the hostilities for the frivolous purpose of commercial advertising.

which time over 2,800 vehicles had been completed. In later years, some of the more severe restrictions were relaxed, with aluminium sheeting for bodywork cladding being permitted from the summer of 1944 and, at the end of that year, the luxury of upholstered seating was once again allowed. Guy and Daimler had now been joined by Bristol, who were permitted to recommence construction in small numbers. Later examples of the Arab from the summer of 1945 were fitted with a single-plate clutch and a new design of gearbox incorporating constant-mesh gears on all speeds. A revision to the gear selection now provided the more conventional layout, with the lower gears to the left of the H

pattern. The revised gearbox provided easier and quicker gear changes and, as an aide-memoire for the driver, the later models were equipped with a red-coloured gear knob.

Despite, or perhaps because of, the very basic design of the utility vehicles, many were to have much longer lives than their designers could have imagined, with many surviving into the 1960s. Furthermore, although Guy had been a successful business during the 1920s and 1930s, the result of many operators experiencing the benefits of the Arab chassis during the years of conflict led to new business for the company in the years following the resumption of normal life.

Despite the shortages of materials and the simplicity of design, the overall appearance of the Arab utility bus is one that remains pleasing to the eye, especially when repainted in the usual livery of the operating bus company.

From the rear, the squared-edge design is apparent, as is the very simple style of the rear dome and the external bracing for the roof. Additional lighting is now fitted to this vehicle; originally, it would have been fitted with a single tail lamp and brake lamp, both placed above the registration plate.

PART-TIME WORKING

With continuing labour shortages and the difficulties of engaging part-time labour due to the structuring of the national labour scheme, Sydney Guy personally instigated a scheme whereby teachers and pupils in the final stages of their education could volunteer to do war work during the school holidays. During term time, part-time woman workers fulfilled the day shift, with businessmen in reserved occupations or otherwise ineligible to join the Forces providing the labour during the evenings and sometimes night shifts. One willing and enthusiastic volunteer for this scheme was a local County Court Judge, whose involvement was no doubt most useful when the Ministry of Employment determined that the schemes were illegal and threatened Sydney Guy with prosecution. However, before matters went further, the Ministry saw that the scheme was beneficial to the war effort, dropped the threat of action against Guy and encouraged similar schemes elsewhere in industry.

Chapter 5

POST-WAR EXPANSION

RETURN TO NORMALITY WITH A NEW ARAB

Having been the beneficiary of the duopoly in the supply of buses during the war years, the Guy Arab was introduced to numerous transport fleets that had not previously experienced Guy products. The rugged simplicity, coupled with a need for minimal maintenance, made it a popular vehicle with operators who struggled to obtain spare parts and a skilled labour force. The bus had also earned itself a reputation of being just about indestructible from a mechanical perspective, although the utility bodies were not to be so long lasting, with many requiring either

rebuilds or complete replacement before the mechanical parts were considered worn beyond the point of repair. Many of the utility vehicles served their original and subsequent owners into the 1960s, with something like 10 per cent of the Arab I chassis being equipped with new bodies, and a quarter of the later Arab IIs being so treated. An alternative approach adopted by some coastal operators was to convert their utility bodied buses into open toppers, always popular with tourists to seaside resorts.

The first new post-war Guy product arrived in 1946 with the introduction of the Guy Arab III, initially as a forward-control, single-deck chassis. Although of similar

ESG652 was delivered to Edinburgh Corporation in September 1948 as its number 739, fitted with a Metro-Cammell thirty-five seat rear-entrance body.

The Green Bus Service was owned and operated by the Whieldon family situated in Uttoxeter in Staffordshire, with operations also in Rugeley and Lichfield, some in cooperation with Midland Red. One of the coaches purchased new by the company is this 1948 Guy Arab III fitted with a thirty-three seat coach body, notable for its curvaceous shape and believed to have been built by Santus Motor Bodies. THE OMNIBUS SOCIETY

outward appearance to the earlier Arabs, by cranking the top radiator stays over the engine, it was possible to lower the bonnet line by 4in (102mm) to improve driver visibility. A welcome return at the time was the polished aluminium radiator, although the profile established with the Arab I was retained and would continue to be fitted to the

Arab exposed radiator chassis until the end of production. Power for the new Arab III came from the reliable Gardner 5LW, with the 6LW optionally available, and in 1948 Guy offered the compact Meadows 6DC630 10.35-litre capacity diesel engine as an option, although this was not to be a popular choice with just a handful being fitted.

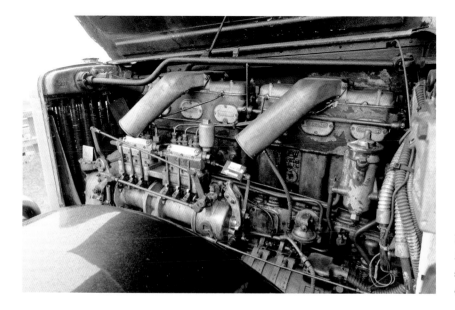

Looking under the bonnet of a Southampton Arab III, the rearranged radiator stays allowed for a lower radiator and consequently a lower bonnet line.

The taller radiator and consequent higher bonnet line was a feature of the early Arabs. Note also the small headlamps.

Although the difference in radiator and bonnet height looks minimal, visibility from the front nearside corner of the vehicle was much improved.

In many respects, the mechanical elements of the Arab III were a continuation of the later Arab II models, with vacuum-assisted hydraulic braking and the newer constant-mesh gearbox and single-plate clutch being fitted. Two rear axle ratios were available: 4.8:1 or 5.6:1. The electrical system was now 12V, with a dynamo rated at 55amp and two 6V batteries providing a capacity of 185amp hours. For the domestic market, a wheelbase of 17ft 6in (5,334mm)

provided for an overall body length of 27ft 6in (8,382mm), while for the export market the wheelbase could be extended to 19ft 6in (5,944mm) on a chassis measuring 30ft 10in (9,398mm) overall to accommodate bodies in accordance with local requirements. Naturally, both right-hand and left-hand driving positions could be accommodated.

A substantial number of single-deck Arab IIIs, both completed vehicles and bare chassis for bodying locally,

Export markets,
especially to the former
Empire countries of
Africa, were important
to Guy Motors. This
is an image of one
Arab III shipped to
Bulawayo, then in
Southern Rhodesia,
now Zimbabwe.
WOLVERHAMPTON CITY
ARCHIVE

were exported, with the African continent receiving large numbers. Within the first three years of the Arab III entering production, around sixty vehicles were shipped to Kenya; twenty to Khartoum in the Sudan; fifteen to Nyasaland (now Malawi); forty to Rhodesia (now Zimbabwe); around twenty-five to Lagos, Nigeria; and over two hundred to South Africa, many of which were fitted with high-capacity bodies seating fifty-three passengers. There were also small numbers to Mozambique and Tanganyika (now Tanzania). Customers in the Netherlands, Norway, Denmark and Portugal were also impressed with the vehicle, placing orders for multiple vehicles.

In the domestic market, around one hundred and fifty vehicles found homes in Scotland, with slightly more than half of these being operated by W. Alexander &

Sons Ltd, and long-term customer Burton-upon-Trent Corporation taking a stock of twenty. Northern General, which prior to the operation of some thirty utility buses had not been a customer of Guy Motors, took a stock of ninety-eight single-deck Arabs into its fleet between 1947–9, with additional orders the following year taking the total to around one hundred and thirty. Of these, the majority were thirty-eight seat forward-entrance service buses, with bodies built by Brush, and ten being coach-built by Windover with thirty seat, front entrance, touring coach bodies. The buses were unusual in that the front bulkhead was moved slightly further forward than normal, resulting in the steering column requiring a steeper rake, but allowing the seating capacity to be increased.

An Arab III with a curious body with
right-hand drive to suit driving on the
left, but with a rear platform entrance
as would be required for driving on the
right. This vehicle was supplied to the
Danish State Railways in 1949.
R. L. WILSON/ONLINE TRANSPORT ARCHIVE

In March 1947, twenty Guy Arab III chassis with thirty-five seat forward-entrance coach bodies by Duple were delivered to Lawson, a subsidiary of the large Alexander concern in Scotland. One of the vehicles in this view, now both in bus livery, has suffered a mishap to its nearside rear corner.

In 1949, five single-deck Guy Arab III buses with Guy's own rear-entrance, thirty-four seat bus bodies were taken into the stock of Wolverhampton Corporation and numbered 561–5. WOLVERHAMPTON CITY ARCHIVE

ELLIOT OR REVERSED ELLIOT?

Almost exclusively, Guy Motors employed front axles of the reversed Elliot style. Elliot and reversed Elliot axle designs have similarities and when employed in heavy vehicles with beam axles describe the method of achieving articulation of the stub axles to allow for steering. In the case of the Elliot axle, the stub axle is fitted with a bush that locates in a yoke forged in the end of the axle beam and articulates around a kingpin, while the reversed Elliot style has the yoke forged into the stub axle assembly that surrounds the bush now located at the end of the axle beam and again secured with a kingpin to provide the steering articulation. Although resulting in a larger mass that needs to be swivelled, the significant advantage of the reversed style is that the steering mechanism is more easily fitted to the larger stub axle sub-assemblies.

The first of the 1949 Wolverhampton single-deck Guys appears to have fallen on hard times in this image, looking rather down at heel and seemingly equipped with a snowplough. The detail of the nearside Guy body is clearly visible. CW

Ten Roe bodied thirty-five seat front-entrance coaches on Arab III chassis entered service with Lancashire United in 1951, one of which has been preserved and features later in this book. MTJ87, originally number 443, was withdrawn in 1964 and was later operated by an independent coach company, Martins, in whose care it is seen in the city centre of Leeds. The location where the coach is parked is now a multistorey car park serving a massive shopping centre. CW

Belfast Corporation was another undertaking that took single-deck Guy Arab III buses into service. Number 286 was one of a large fleet fitted with a locally constructed body by Harkness Coachworks. It remained in service for twenty years, despite being hijacked and used as a barricade during the Troubles. CW

THE ARAB III CHASSIS

Early 1947 saw the launch of an Arab III chassis suitable for double-deck bodywork. This followed the format of the single-deck chassis, including the lowered radiator and bonnet line and the later option of the Meadows engine. For operators wishing to implement the refinements of the Arab III into the earlier utility vehicles, where units were interchangeable, Guy were happy to supply these as spare parts.

Southdown ran a large fleet of Leyland vehicles, but following on from the utility Arabs a number of Arab III vehicles were purchased, including JCD502, which was bodied by Northern Counties and exhibited by them at the 1948 Commercial Motor Show. CW

ABOVE: Wolverhampton took a batch of Arab IIIs with bodywork by Brush in 1949. Seen here from that batch is number 395. The bodies seated fifty-four passengers. CW

LEFT: 559 was delivered a year later, fitted with the familiar Park Royal body. One of the final Arab IIIs to be delivered to Wolverhampton, this one lasted long enough in service to pass to the new West Midlands Passenger Transport Executive in 1969. CW

Between March and July 1950, a fleet of forty Arab III buses fitted with Park Royal low-bridge bodies seating fifty-three passengers, several of which can be seen here parked, was delivered to East Kent Road Car Company. CW

In 1952, Birkenhead Corporation took a batch of East Lancs-bodied fifty-nine seat Arab IIIs into stock. Most remained in service until the end of the 1960s. CW

Guy Motors could rely on committed customer Burton-upon-Trent Corporation to take a fleet of Arab III buses into service. A batch of twelve was supplied in 1950, with bodies by Davies, half of which were to low-bridge format. Most were eventually rebodied, number 18 seen here being fitted with the new Massey Bros high-bridge body in 1960.

BELOW: Southampton Corporation Transport was another committed Guy user, buying nothing but Guy Motors products between 1944–54. LOW217 was one of the last to be supplied and is fitted with a Park Royal body. CW

ABOVE LEFT: Red and White Services took delivery of thirty-three low-bridge Arab IIIs with stylish bodywork by Duple. Fitted with luggage racks and platform doors, the buses found use on some of the longer routes operated. L.1149 is at the Transport Museum in Wythall; the route shown would have started in Gloucester, a journey of about sixty miles.

ABOVE RIGHT: Guy Motors remained creative with their advertising, using an image of RMS *Queen Mary* in its usual operating port of Southampton to promote recent sales to that town.

LEFT: Birch Bros purchased a fleet of six Arab IIIs fitted with distinctively styled bodywork by Willowbrook and fitted with interiors more suitable for touring coaches than buses for use on routes from London to Northamptonshire. AMRTM/GUY ARCHIVE

GUY AS A COACHBUILDER

Early Guy buses were available with Guy-built bodies, but the war years had ended this work. With the huge demand in the immediate post-war years to replace older vehicles and rebody utility vehicles with bodywork more suitable for peacetime, many of the usual suppliers of bus and coach bodies were reporting full order books and were unable to meet the demand for new vehicles or refreshed bodies. This led to Guy Motors returning to the market for complete vehicles, initially for single-deck chassis, for which bus bodies were fitted with either front or rear entrances and a seating capacity varying between thirty-three and thirty-

five passengers. In 1948, an arrangement was made with Park Royal Vehicles for the supply of double-deck frames to allow complete vehicles to be assembled at Fallings Park. The resulting vehicles were indistinguishable from those bodied by Park Royal on Guy chassis. The relationship was to continue until 1953, when Guy Motors ended its role as a passenger vehicle coachwork constructor.

By this time, Park Royal had acquired the Leeds-based business of Charles H. Roe Ltd, another business that would continue to supply many bodies fitted to Guy chassis, with both Park Royal and Roe forming part of the newly created Associated Commercial Vehicles Ltd, which included another well-known commercial vehicle

Inside the body assembly shop at Fallings Park Works, a selection of trolleybuses, double-deck and single-deck motor buses are fitted with Guy bodies. EARDLEY LEWIS PHOTOGRAPHERS

South Yorkshire independent bus operator, Blue Line, took delivery of HWU437 and 438 in 1949. Both were Arab IIIs with 6-cylinder Meadows engines. LWT500 followed in 1952, powered with a Gardner 5LW. All three vehicles were fitted with bodies built by Guy on Park Royal frames. CW

chassis builder, AEC. Despite the obvious rivalry between Guy and AEC, both Park Royal and Roe would continue to provide bodywork for AEC's competitors, including Guy, until the time in the future when all the indigenous British heavy vehicle manufacturers would find themselves under common ownership.

ALL CHANGE FOR TROLLEYBUSES

Trolleybus construction for Guy Motors recommenced in 1947 with a resumption of the six-wheel, 30ft (9,144mm) long BTX and a fleet of seventy chassis being shipped to Belfast to be fitted with bodies locally by Harkness. These stylish machines seated sixty-eight passengers and were fitted with electrical equipment supplied by the General Electric Company. In 1949, a further delivery of smaller BT chassis was supplied locally to Wolverhampton Corporation, with twenty-six being delivered in 1949 and a second batch of twenty-four spread over 1949 and into 1950. These were all powered using British Thomson-Houston Co. equipment and were fitted with fifty-four seat Park Royal bodies in a style very similar to the contemporary motor buses. As far as trolleybuses sold under the Guy name were concerned, these post-war deliveries were to be the very last in a long line.

However, things were not to be that simple. Both the Karrier and Sunbeam businesses had been purchased and merged into the Rootes Brothers empire prior to the war,

with all trolleybus manufacturing during the hostilities centred on Sunbeam's Works at Moorfield, Wolverhampton. Although the Karrier range of commercial vehicles was amalgamated with Rootes' Commer marque of commercials, that was not to be the case with the trolleybus business, which, along with the Sunbeam brand, was sold in 1946 as a going concern to the firm of J. Brockhouse & Co., an engineering business headquartered nearby in West Bromwich. This ownership was not to be long lasting, with Brockhouse reselling the trolleybus business to Guy Motors in September 1948.

This followed an amalgamation two years earlier, when the Associated Engineering Company and Leyland Motors

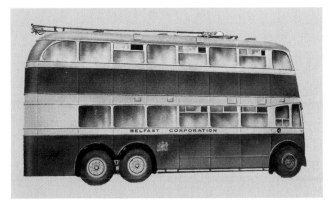

A Works image showing one of the six-wheel Guy BTX trolleybuses shipped to Belfast to be fitted with bodies by Harkness. WOLVERHAMPTON CITY ARCHIVE

One of the final trolleybuses to be produced under the Guy brand was delivered to Wolverhampton Corporation in 1950. Fitted with a Park Royal body, registered FJW648 and wearing fleet number 648, it was withdrawn in 1962 and is seen here in service in Wolverhampton city centre. WOLVERHAMPTON CITY ARCHIVE

established British United Traction Ltd (BUT) as a jointly owned business, with a focus initially on the construction of trolleybuses. Effectively, the only two volume suppliers of trolleybuses to the domestic market and by inference to the British Empire, as it then was, were Guy Motors using the well-established Sunbeam brand, and BUT.

Guy continued production of Sunbeam trolleybuses at the Moorfield Works until 1953, when a new extension to the Fallings Park Works allowed production to be moved to the Guy factory. The Sunbeam models sold exceptionally well in the early 1950s, particularly in export markets, with Guy able to boast in the mid-1950s that there were more Sunbeam trolleybuses in operation in South Africa than all other makes combined. Production was centred around four model types. The MF2B was considered to be a design essentially for overseas use of the single-deck 'transit' design, allowing for capacities of between thirty and forty-four seated passengers and ample space for additional standing loads. Access forward of the front axle, in the centre or rear access, or combinations thereof, were possible to suit local requirements and three different wheelbases were available. Guy's sales literature reported 'important overseas operators' in Adelaide and Brisbane in Australia, plus Coimbra, Portugal.

Despite being considered an export design, the MF2B also found a domestic market, especially for operation in the town of Bournemouth, where the chassis layout accommodated the traditional rear open platform and front platform fitted with driver-operated doors used for exiting passengers, and in the city of Kingston-upon-Hull, where a similar dual-door arrangement was employed, although in the case of the Hull vehicles, the rear door was placed ahead of the rear axle, predating the style and layout of modern buses. Similar to this first model was the MF2R, the major difference being that the traction motor was mounted at the rear of the chassis, which provided a better weight distribution when high-capacity bodies were fitted.

The S7 was described as being the latest development of the Sunbeam three-axle chassis, first introduced in 1938 and it effectively replaced the Guy BTX after the acquisition of Sunbeam. Again available in various wheelbase dimensions, allowing for bodywork of a length determined by local regulations, those for the UK market could accommodate bodies of up to 30ft (9,144mm) in length, then the maximum for a six-wheel, three-axle bus, and could accommodate up to seventy seated passengers. Fleets of these vehicles were operated by the Municipal undertakings in Reading, Huddersfield and Newcastle. Two additional variations were available: the S7A was designed for bodywork of 7ft 6in (2,286mm), of interest to operators whose routes covered narrow city

ABOVE: The first trolleybus to run in Brisbane, Australia, was this Sunbeam MF2B fitted with this large-capacity, single-deck dual-entrance body.

One of the last trolleybuses to be delivered to the home market, Bournemouth took a number of MF2B chassis fitted with bodies by Weymann, complete with the classic Bournemouth features of forward doors, rear platform and twin staircases. Now preserved, YLJ286 was new in 1959.

streets; and the S7B, which featured a forward chassis extension suitable for front entrance.

Introduced in 1954, the F4A was listed as a two-axle chassis suitable for single- or double-deck bodies, with a capacity of up to sixty-two passengers, and was promoted as being an enhancement of earlier models that had been supplied in large numbers both at home and overseas. The sales and marketing literature placed great emphasis on operations in Johannesburg, Durban and Pretoria in South Africa; and Perth, Australia, where a new fleet of fifty single-deck vehicles was promoted, and a fleet in operation in Georgetown, Penang (Malaysia), emphasizing that the vehicles were robust enough to operate in every condition of service. This model remained in production until 1961, when, with the MF2B, it was to be amongst the very last trolleybus chassis manufactured for the domestic market.

A fleet of MF2B trolleybuses with stylish dual-entrance bodies by Charles Roe entered service with Hull Corporation in 1953, the year of the Coronation of HM Queen Elizabeth II, in commemoration of which the vehicles were always known as 'Coronations'. MARCUS EAVIS/ ONLINE TRANSPORT ARCHIVE

NRH101, the first of the Coronation fleet, was shown at the Commercial Motor Show. Here in service in Hull, this rear view shows the retaining wires attached to the trolley masts, something that was unusual in the UK. HARRY LUFF/ONLINE TRANSPORT ARCHIVE

Another view of NRH101, seen
here in Paragon Street, outside
the City Hall making an orbit of
Queen Victoria's statue. The two
sets of doors are visible, as is the
distinctive livery that was used
to paint Hull's public service
vehicles. HARRY LUFF/ONLINE
TRANSPORT ARCHIVE

ABOVE LEFT: Reading Corporation operated a fleet of twelve Sunbeam S7 trolleybuses, with Park Royal bodies seating sixty-eight and
fitted with platform doors. New in 1950, number 181 was withdrawn in 1968 with the closure of the Reading system and has been
preserved. COLIN RADFORD

ABOVE RIGHT: The first of a batch of ten Sunbeam S7A vehicles fitted with East Lancs Coachbuilders' seventy-two seat rear-entrance
bodies, constructed to a width of 7ft 6in (2,286mm) to deal with narrow streets, was delivered to Huddersfield Corporation in 1959
and withdrawn in 1968. These were the final six-wheeled trolleybuses built for service in the UK.

Built for Derby Corporation almost at the end of construction for the home market, here is preserved Sunbeam F4A with Charles Roe body SCH237, seen while awaiting service at the East Anglia Transport Museum.

NATIONALIZATION

One of the actions following the election of Clement Atlee's new Labour Government in 1945 was the nationalization of transport in the United Kingdom with the 1947 Transport Act. Primarily remembered as the action that resulted in British Railways, the new legislation had an impact on bus operations, with both benefits and risks to Guy Motors. There had already been a pattern of mergers occurring among bus operators, with them forming into three distinct groups. One group owned by British Electric Traction was a huge conglomerate with other interests in such diverse businesses as laundry and linen rental; another was the Scottish Motor Traction Group; while the third was the Tilling Group. Major shareholders in each of the groups included the 'big four' railway companies and therefore, following nationalization of the railways, a significant ownership of bus companies fell under the control of the newly established British Transport Commission. The Tilling Group and Scottish Motor Traction Group sold their remaining shareholdings to the Government at the beginning of 1949. BET remained independent, but with some Government shareholding.

Tilling had acquired both Bristol Commercial Vehicles and Eastern Coach Works (ECW) in the 1930s and as a result of the group now being under public ownership, the supply of Bristol/ECW vehicles was restricted to the nationalized operators, who were actively discouraged from purchasing outside the group. Thus, following nationalization, Guy's home market became the municipal operators, companies within the BET group, and independent operators for whom purchasing Bristol chassis was now not even an option.

With the nationalization of much of the road transport industry, the Eastern Coach Works and Bristol chassis combination was restricted to the publicly owned operators. This former Southern Vectis Bristol LD6G with standard ECW body is representative of vehicles that were seen all over the UK.

LONGER VEHICLES AT LAST PERMITTED

The limits on bus body lengths had been enforced since the regulations contained within the 1930 Road Traffic Act had been enacted, although dispensation for vehicle widths of up to 8ft (2,439mm) had been allowed, except in the Metropolitan district, where separate regulations persisted. In 1952, Walsall, then in the county of Staffordshire and now part of the West Midlands conurbation, appointed a new General Manager for its passenger transport services. He was Mr Ronald Edgley Cox, who quickly established a reputation for innovative thinking. An early trolleybus purchase in his regime was for a single, six-wheeled vehicle fitted with two staircases and a seated conductor, who collected fares as the passengers entered the vehicle.

Cox's policy in general was to purchase anything that was new or different, in limited numbers, and for subsequent purchases to try something totally different. It was therefore not surprising when, in 1954, a new fleet of trolleybuses was required to replace life-expired pre-war vehicles, and to expand the network, something very different would emerge. Edgley Cox was able successfully to petition the Ministry of Transport to allow a special

The first vehicles of 30ft (9,144mm) length on two axles to be permitted in the UK were Sunbeam S4A trolleybuses fitted with Willowbrook bodies that were operated in Walsall. Number 862 is seen operating at the Black Country Living Museum in Dudley, West Midlands.

A profile view of Walsall's S4A trolleybuses reveals the additional length permitted.

dispensation for vehicles of 30ft (9,144mm) in length to be operated on two axles; the first time that this had been permitted in the UK. An order of twenty-two Sunbeam F4A chassis was placed for delivery over two years and to be fitted with seventy-seat double-deck, rear-entrance bodywork constructed by Willowbrook. The bodywork was distinctively different to anything else previously seen and soon gained the nickname of 'goldfish bowl' on account of its bulbous shape. However, the lasting benefit of these buses was to pave the way for the relaxation of the length limit to allow 30ft buses on two axles to be permitted in normal operation.

ARAB III ENHANCEMENTS

1948 increased the options available for potential users of both single-deck and double-deck Arab IIIs. The option of the Meadows engine has already been mentioned, but other options now included a preselective gearbox and air brakes. An early customer for all these options was Newport Corporation and a production chassis from the batch being built for that undertaking was subject to a

test by *Commercial Motor* in December 1948. The new Guy–Meadows engine was met with enthusiasm, with emphasis being placed on its modular assembly, resulting in it being possible to install the engine into a half-cab chassis such that the ancillaries were accessible from the bonnet side irrespective of whether the chassis was set up for right-hand or left-hand drive feature. This was demonstrated to good effect at the Commercial Motor Show, where a Meadows-equipped export model Arab III chassis was displayed.

The engine, of 'square dimensions', having equal bore and stroke of 5.11in (130mm), was set to develop 115bhp at 1,800rpm and 390lb ft torque at 1,000rpm in the Arab III installation. Transmission, via a fluid flywheel, was taken to a Wilson preselective gearbox mounted in the traditional Guy fashion approximately halfway between the front bulkhead and the rear axle. It was reported that just minimal modification was required to accommodate the new gearbox. Gear selection was by way of a conventional gear lever, with the gear positions shown in the conventional H pattern and operation by way of a foot pedal with air assistance to ease the work of the driver. The braking system was either of Clayton Dewandre or

Guy's sales brochure featured a number of stylized images of the company's products, including this Meadows-powered Arab III touring coach.

GUY ARAB III MEADOWS-ENGINED PASSENGER CHASSIS WITH AIR BRAKING AND PRESELECTIVE GEARBOX SPECIFICATION

Layout	Forward-control four-wheel chassis for double-deck bodywork	**Axles**	
Engine	Henry Meadows & Co.	Front	H section
Bore and stroke	Bore: 5.11in (130mm), stroke: 5.11in (130mm)	Rear	4.6:1
Capacity	10.35 litres	**Electrical system**	24V or 12V electrical system, as specified by customer
Valves	2 valves per cylinder		
		Brakes	
Transmission	Fluid flywheel	Type	Foot brake operating drums on all wheels; compressed air operated
Gearbox	Wilson type epicyclic, manufactured by Guy Motors		Front drums 17in diameter × 3.5in wide (432 × 89mm)
Overall ratios:			Rear drums 16.25in diameter × 6.5in wide (412.75 × 165mm)
1st	4.2:1	Handbrake	Conventional lever, operating on rear wheels only
2nd	2.37:1		
3rd	1.57:1		
4th	1:1		
Reverse	6.09:1	**Dimensions**	As earlier Guy Arab chassis
Suspension and steering			
Suspension	Semi-elliptic front and rear		
Steering	Marles steering box		

Westinghouse construction and consisted of an engine-mounted compressor, chassis-mounted air-supply tank and actuating cylinders for each wheel; the rear brake cylinders were mounted on the chassis sides, while at the front, the cylinders were fitted above the kingpins.

An Arab III on Trial in London

During a period when the standard London bus was rapidly becoming the AEC Regent fitted with the familiar RT body, Guy Motors supplied a solitary Arab III fitted with the standard Guy-constructed Park Royal body. Powered by a Meadows 10.35-litre engine developing 130bhp, providing a 15bhp advantage over the engine fitted to the RT and using a preselective gearbox, this vehicle was different to the utility Arabs that London Transport was rapidly withdrawing and the standardized buses that were taking their place, filling the streets of the capital. Although Leyland also built chassis for London Transport

and other coachbuilders provided bodies, these were all to the general style of the standard RT, while the Guy was unique in terms of both motive power and bodywork.

Internally, the seats were typical of the style fitted to the Park Royal-bodied Guy Arabs being supplied in large numbers to municipal operators across the country and upholstered in the same moquette as used on the RT. As a unique vehicle, its use was limited and confined to two routes: one operating between Peckham and Nunhead in south-east London, a service that could be operated by a solitary vehicle; and after moving to Enfield in 1953, following a comprehensive overhaul, on a short shuttle service between Ponders End and Chingford.

The bus carried the fleet number G436 and was registered KGK 981. Following withdrawal from service in 1955, the bus was sold for further service in Yugoslavia. Guy built a second chassis with modifications to the body mounting points so that the standard Park Royal RT body could be fitted, but London Transport could not be convinced to take up this offer.

KGK981 was a Meadows-engined Arab III with Guy body supplied to London Transport with the hope that further sales might follow. It remained as a unique vehicle in the fleet and so was doomed to have a short life. The public house in the background, 'The Paget Arms', was located opposite the Guy Motors Works. ASTON MANOR ROAD TRANSPORT MUSEUM/GUY ARCHIVE

Only the application of the London Transport name distinguishes G436 from the large fleet of Park Royal-bodied Arab IIIs then being delivered. ASTON MANOR ROAD TRANSPORT MUSEUM/GUY ARCHIVE

The interior was a hybrid of London Transport and standard Guy features. ASTON MANOR ROAD TRANSPORT MUSEUM/GUY ARCHIVE

Chapter 6

REPOSITIONING THE ENGINE AND THE NEW ARAB IV

For single-deck buses and coaches, the traditional front-mounted engine, while it provided for ease of access for maintenance, restricted the maximum carrying capacity of the vehicle within the specified overall length. Despite the regulations on vehicle lengths being slowly relaxed, a better solution was to set the front axle slightly to the rear of the driver with a passenger entrance under the driver's supervision and to relocate the engine. The space required for an entrance was less than the space taken up by the engine and would allow for extra seating capacity within the permitted length. The obvious place to locate the engine was under the floor. Although some designs had been proposed during the 1930s, the pressure to rebuild the bus fleets in the late 1940s had postponed further developments.

Guy Motors were very quick to announce their offering of this new advance at the 1950 Commercial Motor Show, where it was shown in competition with similar underfloor bus and coach chassis. It was a strong year for chassis developments, with nearly thirty new chassis being shown to the industry for the first time, including models from AEC, Maudslay and Crossley, all powered by an AEC 9.6-litre 6-cylinder engine, Leyland and Sentinel. Guy were the only supplier to display a chassis designed for underfloor engine mounting to utilize the Gardner engine, as a result of work undertaken jointly by the two companies to adapt the LW series of engines to horizontal mounting, with the resulting HLW model range being announced by Gardner at the same show.

Guy emphasized that a key advantage of the Arab UF (for 'underfloor') chassis was the commonality of the majority of components with the conventional front-engined models. The engine was also, to the extent that the transformation to horizontal mounting made possible, common in design with the vertical models; the major differences being the sump, which was a new aluminium casting, and an extended shaft to drive a cooling fan intended to be mounted remotely from the engine.

The chassis arrangements for the new underfloor-engined Arab. The substantial and robust construction is evident, as is the raised section of the chassis rails to accommodate the engine.
ASTON MANOR ROAD TRANSPORT MUSEUM/GUY ARCHIVE

This second image of an underfloor-engined Arab chassis shows the rear dropped to provide for a large luggage compartment for a touring coach. ASTON MANOR ROAD TRANSPORT MUSEUM/GUY ARCHIVE

The 6HLW engine shared the same bore and stroke as the 6LW, but with revisions the power output had increased to 112bhp at 1,700rpm and 358lb ft torque at 1,280rpm. The company exhibited two Arab UFs at the show, one being a bare chassis and the second a completed vehicle fitted with a forty-seat bus body built by Guy on frames supplied by Park Royal under the agreement that was still in place between the two companies. Initially, deliveries were exclusively 6-cylinder engines with a preselective gearbox and air brakes, but it was announced that a lower powered 5HLW engine,

constant-mesh gearbox and triple-servo vacuum brakes would be available to suit customers' specific requirements. The home-market models featured a 16ft 4in (4,978mm) wheelbase for a 30ft (9,144mm) maximum length, while the export model could be specified with a wheelbase of 17ft 6in (5,334mm) to support an overall body length of 35ft (10,668mm) and in both cases, 7ft 6in (2,286mm) and 8ft (2,438mm) width chassis were specified.

In common with the other early underfloor chassis, the Arab UF was heavily over-engineered, with a degree

A Guy Arab UF was on display at the 1950 Commercial Motor Show fitted with a Guy forty-seat front-entrance bus body. Afterwards, it was given the registration GUY 3 and became a demonstrator for the model, before being sold to the Yorkshire bus firm of Kitchen and Son, then finding its way to another Yorkshire independent, Samuel Ledgard, when some public service routes were taken over. WOLVERHAMPTON CITY ARCHIVE

of robustness that was in excess of that required for the domestic market, but this over-engineering provided a feature that was to make it very suitable for the less-than-perfect road surfaces of many export markets. An unfortunate result of this over-cautiousness in the engineering resulted in a single-deck UF bus weighing much the same as a contemporary double-decker, a situation that was quickly rectified with the launch of a revised model in 1952 employing more alloy castings and a lighter construction. Quite logically, this new light-

weight model was given the name of LUF. Both UF and LUF continued in production alongside each other until 1959, with the UF becoming predominantly an export model.

Guy Motors finished a UF chassis with a front entrance forty-seat Park Royal bus body, which, having been appropriately registered 'GUY 3', was used as a demonstrator and was tested by the press, before eventually finding its way to the fleet of Samuel Ledgard. The specifics of this vehicle appear in the table below.

GUY ARAB UF GARDNER 6HLW-ENGINED PASSENGER CHASSIS WITH AIR BRAKING AND PRESELECTIVE GEARBOX SPECIFICATION

Layout	Forward-control four-wheel underfloor engine chassis for single-deck bodywork	**Electrical system**	24V system, 185AH batteries
Engine	Gardner 6HLW	**Brakes**	
Bore and stroke	Bore: 4.5in (114mm), stroke: 6in (152mm)	Type	Foot brake operating drums on all wheels; compressed air operated Front drums 16.5in diameter × 4in wide (419 × 102mm)
Capacity	8.4 litres		Rear drums 16.25in diameter ×
Valves	2 valves per cylinder		6.5in wide (412.75 × 165mm)
Power	112bhp at 1,700rpm	Handbrake	Conventional lever, operating on
Torque	358ft lb at 1,280rpm		rear wheels only
Transmission	Fluid flywheel		
Gearbox	Wilson type epicyclic, manufactured by Guy Motors	**Dimensions (chassis)**	
		Overall length	29ft 3.125in (8,915mm)
Overall ratios:		Overall width	7ft 9.5in (2,375mm)
1st	4.2:1	Wheelbase	16ft 4in (4,978mm)
2nd	2.37:1	Unladen weight (demonstrator)	4 tons 15cwt (4.7 tonnes) chassis only; 7 tons 19cwt (7.9 tonnes) with Park Royal body
3rd	1.57:1		
4th	1:1		
5th	0.755:1	Nominal operational weight with full load	10 tons 7cwt (10.3 tonnes)
Reverse	6.09:1		
		Fuel tank capacity	35gal (159ltr)
Suspension and steering			
Suspension	Semi-elliptic front and rear, hydraulic shock absorbers	**Performance**	
		Acceleration	0–40mph (0–64km/h) achieved in 50.3sec when tested by *Commercial Motor*
Steering	Marles cam and double roller steering box		
		Fuel economy	13.6mpg (20.8/100km) touring, reducing to 8.2mpg (34.5/100km) in typical urban bus operations with four stops per mile (figures from *Commercial Motor* test)
Axles			
Front	I section, set back 5ft 4.125in (1,628mm) from front of chassis		
Rear	Final drive ratio 4.8:1		

SOUTHAMPTON CORPORATION TRANSPORT – A LOYAL GUY CUSTOMER

Having been an early customer for the original Guy Arab in 1934 and operating a fleet of fifty Arab IIs, all but the first five having Park Royal bodies, Southampton Corporation Transport built up a substantial fleet of almost one hundred and fifty Park Royal-bodied 6LW-powered Guy Arab IIIs that were to remain in service into the mid-1970s, ultimately becoming the largest single operator of the type and featuring in an advertisement by Guy Motors. Even several years after the later Arab IV was announced to the market, SCT continued to purchase the known and trusted Arab III.

It was therefore no surprise that the Corporation purchased a fleet of twelve Arab UFs in 1952. Half of these were fitted with Park Royal bodies featuring dual doors and seating just twenty-six passengers with substantial space for up to twenty-six standing passengers, for which a special dispensation had been obtained, the regulations usually only permitting eight standing. The intention was that during peak times the buses would carry a conductor who sat at a small desk located over the rear nearside wheels to collect fares and operate the rear boarding doors while the driver operated the front exit doors. Outside peak times, the capacity was restricted to twenty-six passengers, with the rear door out of service and the driver collecting fares.

One of the UFs that were delivered in 1952, but not fitted with bodies until 1955, JOW924, fleet number 251, rests at the depot next to one of the many Arab IIIs that were operated. This bus remained in the fleet until 1973. CW

JOW919 was numerically the third of the UFs to be supplied to Southampton in 1952. It was withdrawn in 1963 and is seen here in service with Wheildon (Green Bus) parked next to another former Southampton vehicle, a Park Royal-bodied Arab II. CW

The arrangement was not considered a success and the buses were quickly modified to conventional seating, now accommodating thirty-six seats. The second batch of chassis, having been held in store, were fitted with Park Royal dual-door bodies, again with seating for thirty-six, in 1955. The early batch were withdrawn in 1963, with the remaining vehicles modified again to remove the rear entrance and increase the seating capacity to thirty-nine, in which condition they were to continue operating until withdrawal. Two examples of the fleet were withdrawn in 1964; a further example left in 1968 and the remaining three survived until 1971. The last vehicle to have been delivered ended its life with the Corporation, having been converted to transport for the city's Welfare Service.

The final Southampton UF was withdrawn from bus duties in 1968 and found further use after conversion with the city's Welfare Service. The bus was saved for preservation and is undergoing long-term restoration. CW

A six-wheel version of the UF was built in 1954 for Rhodesian Railways, powered by a 6HLW engine adjusted for running at an average altitude of 4,000ft (1,219m) and measuring 35ft (10,668mm) overall with an 18ft 4in (5,588mm) wheelbase. Power was transmitted via a five-speed non-overdrive preselective gearbox, and a manually operated intermediate differential lock was fitted. The body was fitted with three compartments: an unglazed compartment located over the engine for the carriage of mail; a forward first-class saloon fitted with nine upholstered seats, described at the time as being 'for Europeans'; and at the rear a further saloon fitted with wooden slatted seats for forty-one passengers.

The UF and LUF gained widespread acceptance in the market as a single-deck service bus, as a coach on long-distance services and as a luxury coach for touring. One substantial customer for the new underfloor coach, in addition to a fleet of low-bridge Arab III buses fitted with distinctive bodies by Duple intended for long-stage carriage routes, was the Red & White Group with operations in South Wales, the Welsh and English border counties, the South Midlands and the area bordering Hampshire and Berkshire.

Red & White came under public ownership from 1950 when the management voluntarily negotiated the sale of the business to the British Transport Commission, but honoured orders placed with Guy for thirty-three Arab IIIs to be delivered between 1949–51, two of which were operated by subsidiary business Newbury & District, and an additional fifteen high-bridge vehicles operated by other companies within the Red & White Group.

Orders had also been placed for a fleet of twenty-five single-deck Arab III chassis to be fitted with coach bodies for express services. An agreement was reached to delay the actual delivery until the new underfloor chassis was available and deliveries commenced in August 1952. The initial batch of twenty-one was fitted with stylish thirty-seven seat front-entrance Duple Roadmaster bodies, with fourteen operating in main fleet Red & White livery and the balance being finished in the style of United Welsh. The second batch of four vehicles was intended to have been bodied by Lydney Coachworks with a forty-one seat centre-entrance style based on a Leyland design, but with the closure of the Lydney Works, the vehicles were finished at BBW in Brislington. These vehicles were

Parked outside the Works, this chassis is of the type supplied to Rhodesian Railways and shows to good effect the simple but robust construction of the UF chassis. WOLVERHAMPTON CITY ARCHIVE

HWN370 was one of the initial batch of Guy Arab UFs supplied in 1952 with Duple Roadmaster thirty-seven seat coach touring bodies to Red & White services, this example being one of the batch allocated to the fleet of United Welsh. Following its withdrawal and sale, it found its way to the Green Bus operation of Wheildons. THE OMNIBUS SOCIETY

Eight UFs were delivered to Central SMT in Scotland fitted with this style of coachwork by Walter Alexander, seating forty-one with a central entrance. GVD 44 was numerically the last in the batch and had found service in a new life at the time this photograph was taken. CW

BELOW RIGHT: Although supplied later than the Seagull-bodied LUFs mentioned in the text, 1294RE was one of two Arab LUFs supplied to Harper Brothers of Hayes Heath for the 1959 season fitted with a later style front-entrance Burlingham Seagull body.

initially allocated to the South Midland fleet, then transferred to the main Red & White fleet in 1960. The last of the Red & White group's UFs were retired from service in 1967, having been downgraded, like many of the others in the batch, to dual-purpose vehicles suitable for use either as buses or coaches.

Loyal Guy customer Lancashire United added an order for seven Roe coach-bodied UFs seating thirty-nine passengers, delivered in 1952, then followed by a further six in 1954 with dual-purpose forty-seat Weymann bodies. In Scotland, members of the Scottish Motor Group purchased UFs with bodies by Walter Alexander & Co. for both local and long distance services.

One of the more stylish coach bodies of the era was the Seagull designed and built by Burlingham in the coastal resort of Blackpool. Local to the Guy factory, independent operator Don Everall Ltd purchased a fleet of fourteen LUFs fitted with the Seagull body as part of a fleet renewal in 1954, also taking similarly bodied vehicles from Leyland and AEC.

In the case of the Guy vehicles, these supplemented similar UF models that had been acquired earlier and an article in *Commercial Motor* commented that the weight reduction amounted to some 30cwt (1,524kg), with average fuel economy of 15.5mpg (18.3ltr/100km) and reduced operating costs resulting from lower brake and tyre wear. As was usual for Guy, the export market remained important, with a fleet of 35ft (10,668mm) long UFs bodied with forty-nine seat, dual-entrance bus

bodies being supplied to the city of Durban, with similar vehicles also being supplied to Hong Kong.

A curious sale was to Aldershot & District, which had a fleet of around twenty low-bridge Arab IIs, most of which were rebodied with either Weymann or East Lancs bodies during the 1950s. The company purchased only

The centre emergency door provides a connection to the earlier Seagull bodies, which were fitted with a centre entrance.

LEFT: Missing the large exposed radiator, a new location was required for the familiar Guy mascot and badge, now located between the grilles providing cooling air for the radiator.

BELOW LEFT: The Seagull body could be fitted to other chassis, including those built by AEC and Leyland, but the Guy Motors badge and mascot confirms the origin.

locally manufactured Dennis vehicles until 1954, but in 1953 a single LUF fitted with a forty-one seat rear-entrance bus body by East Lancs was acquired. Aldershot & District subsequently shifted its allegiance to AEC for underfloor single-deck chassis, so perhaps found the Guy to be unsuitable.

During the 1950s and 1960s, a staple part of long-distance coach travel in the UK was operated under the banner of Associated Motorways, with its operations based on the coach station in Cheltenham, home to Black & White Motorways Ltd. Associated Motorways itself did not operate any services, but was formed in 1934 to minimize duplication of services, with each member company agreeing to operate certain services, and also a revenue pooling scheme. Black & White

The unique Guy LUF to operate for Aldershot & District is seen here. Delivered in 1953, it carried a forty-one seat rear-entrance bus body, the rear entrance being a curious choice for an underfloor-engined bus. CW

Photographed at Victoria Coach Station in London, PAD184 was one of a batch of twelve Willowbrook-bodied Guy LUFs new in 1955 and forming part of the fleet of Black & White Motorways. The centre-door coaches seated thirty-seven. THE OMNIBUS SOCIETY

Motorways operated an eclectic fleet of vehicles, with examples from almost every builder of chassis and bodywork during its lifetime. Thirty-one Arab LUFs were operated, with deliveries beginning in 1954 when fifteen vehicles fitted with Duple bodies were acquired, followed the next year by eleven and in 1956 a further five, all bodied by Willowbrook. All thirty-one vehicles seated thirty-seven and featured centre entrances.

THE CRELLIN DUPLEX

The Crellin Duplex coach adopted the ideas of Mr George Crellin, a consulting engineer with a practice specializing in matters relating to vehicle construction to maximize the number of passengers that could be accommodated within a vehicle of 27ft 6in (8,382mm) length and with a height of 11ft 6in (3,505mm), between

Another approach to increase capacity was the Duplex coach, a prototype for which was designed and patented by Mr George Crellin on a Guy Arab III chassis. THE STILLTIME COLLECTION

BELOW LEFT: Although the prototype Crellin Duplex coach on the Guy chassis no longer exists, one Duplex coach built on a Leyland Tiger Cub chassis has survived and is seen here at the East Anglia Transport Museum in 2017. The curious seating arrangements can be seen clearly.

that of a conventional single-decker and a low-bridge double-decker. The unique feature of the design was to adopt a 'brick wall' approach to seating, with seats arranged facing each other in groups of four in the style of a railway carriage and with upper seating arranged so that the leg space sat between the seat backs of the lower deck. A single gangway gave access to all seats, with it being necessary to mount a small step to access the upper tiers. Windows were positioned between each group of seats to give good visibility and ventilation for passengers.

A prototype was constructed on an Arab III double-deck chassis with a rearward extension to accommodate the full vehicle length, while revised suspension dealt with the reduced gross weight and a single-decker rear axle provided a lower ratio to give a higher top speed in keeping with the vehicle's intended use as a coach. The front styling was curvaceous in the extreme, giving good forward visibility for passengers. Built by the Lincs Trailer Company in Scunthorpe, who had been appointed as sole licensee of the system, the prototype seating forty-six was operated by Falga Motor Company, who were based in Preston. The prototype was the only one to be built on a Guy chassis, but several similar bodies of less striking design were fitted to other chassis. The prototype no longer survives, but one similar vehicle on a Leyland chassis has been preserved.

At first glance, the seating arrangements of the Crellin Duplex could easily be mistaken for a railway carriage.

The exterior of the Duplex coach has been described as being similar to a delivery van or horsebox. The design was not to prove popular, with only around twenty being built on a variety of different chassis.

THE BIRMINGHAM STANDARD INTRODUCES THE ARAB IV

The city of Birmingham was one that did not fully embrace the trolleybus, having only five routes and closing in 1951; by this time the decision had been taken to replace and expand the system with motor buses, requiring a substantial purchase of new vehicles to be made. Although Birmingham Corporation had some limited experience with Guy products, its supplier of choice was Daimler, with incursions into the fleet by Leyland and AEC being made during the 1930s, with a significant fleet of eighty-four utility Arabs being taken into the fleet.

Birmingham's Transport Department had its own ideas on the design of the modern double-decker bus, which included a new style for the front of the bus with an enclosed radiator and a staircase as straight as possible, even at the cost of seating capacity. The first vehicles to be delivered to this new design were supplied in 1950 by Crossley, who designated the model as model DD42/7, supplying a fleet of completed vehicles incorporating the requirements of the Transport Department and seating fifty-four in total, with thirty upstairs and twenty-four on the lower deck. These were followed between 1950–53 by 300 Guy Arabs bodied locally by Metro-Cammell to the Birmingham standard style and one by Saunders-Roe.

To ease the load on the driver, the newly introduced preselective gearbox was specified. In the general market, the bus was sold as the Arab IV, with the option of the new style frontal treatment, or if required the retention of the traditional polished radiator, which now finished flush with the front of the driver's cab irrespective of which engine was installed. Despite the introduction of the new model, the earlier Arab III remained in production until 1953, with the final Arab IIIs being delivered to Southampton Corporation Transport in 1954.

In conjunction with the introduction of the Arab IV, a single-deck version for overseas markets was announced in two wheelbase lengths suitable for bodywork of 30ft (9,144mm) or 33ft (10,058mm).

ABOVE LEFT: The classic style of the Birmingham bus is seen here in this Metro-Cammell-bodied Guy Arab IV, now housed at the Transport Museum at Wythall. The design swept in a new style with the removal of exposed radiators.

LEFT: The frontal appearance was either the 'new look' or a 'tin front', depending on viewpoint, but it presented a clean and up-to-date appearance to the front of the Birmingham Standards. Guy's Indian Chief badge sits above the city's coat of arms.

ABOVE: As was usual on buses, the driver's cab was a Spartan environment. The steeply raked windscreen, fitted to reduce the dazzle from the sun, has little impact on the driver's field of view. The tachograph is a recent fitting.

LEFT: A feature of the Birmingham design was the straight staircase. Although it could be safer to use when the vehicle was approaching or leaving a stop, it did reduce the number of seats available.

ARAB IV GENERAL SPECIFICATION

Extracted from the promotional material for the new Arab IV, the following table lists the key features of the double-deck chassis.

The standard specification of the 'Arab' MK IV double-deck chassis includes many alternatives, so that every requirement of the operator may be met. The 26ft overall length chassis is offered with either 5LW or 6LW Gardner or 6DC630 Meadows oil engines. In view of the higher gross weight, the 5LW engine is not available in the 30ft version. A Guy-built Wilson pre-selector gearbox is available as an alternative to the constant-mesh unit.

FRAME. The main frame is of carbon-manganese channel section, well braced with channel and tubular cross-members. Fitted bolts are used throughout with their obvious advantages over riveted construction.

CONSTANT-MESH GEARBOX. Front and rear mountings provided with rubber bushes, which assist in insulating noise from the chassis and ensure correct alignment. All forward gears are in constant mesh and are engaged by dog clutches.

FRICTION CLUTCH. Single-plate clutch with cast-iron wearing plate bolted to flywheel. Air space provided between wearing plate and flywheel.

SILENCER AND EXHAUST. Extra large silencer and 3in diameter exhaust system. Front pipe fitted with intermediate flexible connection.

FLUID FLYWHEEL AND PRESELECTIVE EPICYCLIC GEARBOX. Fluid flywheel and four-speed preselective epicyclic gearbox with mechanical or air-operated gear change.

STEERING. Marles cam and double roller type 28.5:1 ratio, which gives very smooth and easy steering, together with a light castor return action. 21in diameter steering wheel.

PROPELLER SHAFTS. Hardy Spicer shafts with needle roller universal joints. Metal shields provided over intermediate and rear joints to eliminate oil splash.

FRONT AXLE. Front axle of the reversed Elliot type, with 'I'-section axle beam of alloy steel.

REAR AXLE. Drop forged casing, underslung worm, with differential offset to side of chassis.

RADIATOR. Exposed Type. Distinctively designed, grilled tube type, with brightly polished exterior.
Enclosed type. The radiator has no appearance factor controlling the design, thereby permitting simple but extremely robust construction. Cooling element of the Withnell type, assembled in special corrosion-resistant rubber ferrules.

BRAKES. The Bendix-Westinghouse air-pressure system is fitted. A 10cu ft per minute, twin cylinder, belt-driven compressor is driven from the transmission.

With many bus operators being very conservative in their outlook, although not explicitly listed in the sales literature, one of the options that remained available to meet 'every requirement of the operator' was vacuum-operated braking. This was of the triple servo type utilizing a single servo unit to operate the rear brakes and two further servo units for the front, one operating each of the front wheels.

A conservative choice for Southdown resulted in a fleet of Arab IV buses with exposed radiators, manual transmission and vacuum brakes equipped with fifty-nine seat Park Royal bodies fitted with platform doors being taken into service in 1956. These followed a smaller batch the previous year and were to be the final Guy vehicles to be purchased by the company. CW

1960 saw the arrival of the final five Guy buses to be delivered to Exeter. Fitted with fifty-seven seat bodies by Massey Brothers, the exposed radiator was a distinctive if rather old-fashioned feature for the time.

Seen outside the Royal Pavilion in Brighton, OUF514, one of the batch of Arab IV vehicles delivered to Southdown, shows screens for service 31 that will take it along the south coast to Portsmouth and its eventual terminus at Southsea, South Parade Pier, a route often stated as being the longest normally operated stage carriage service in the UK. AMRTM/GUY ARCHIVE

TIN FRONTS OR NEW LOOK?

The Birmingham Standard design introduced a trend that led to the removal of the traditional upright polished radiator from the front of the bus. Many Guy Arab IV customers specified the 'new look' front to give an up-to-date appearance to their vehicles, while some rebuilds of earlier utility vehicles, especially those for Edinburgh Corporation, were fitted with another style of 'tin front' that covered the entire front of the vehicle below the driver's windscreen. A further variation on the theme came about with

a frontal treatment applied to buses supplied to Johannesburg, with an even more curvaceous front with a different treatment to the grille area. This style became an option for domestic operators if required and was known as the 'Johannesburg front'. On the other hand, some operators remained steadfastly committed to the traditional exposed polished radiator and continued to specify this for fitting to their vehicles, while others opted for a frontal design boxing in the space between the engine cover and canopy to give a completely flat front to their vehicles in the style of the underfloor-engined single-deckers.

1959 saw ten Arab IVs with 30ft (9,144mm) Northern Counties rear-entrance bodies with seating for seventy-three delivered to Lancashire United and numbered 18 to 27. Number 19 is seen in service, awaiting its next departure. CW

ABOVE: Built towards the end of Arab IV production and delivered early in 1962 with a fifty-nine seat body built by Charles Roe, Pontypridd Urban District Council selected the 'Johannesburg front' for this bus. It remained in service until 1977. CW

LEFT: Number 21, part of the batch of ten Arab IVs supplied in 1959 to Lancashire United, is seen on display at the North West Road Transport Museum in St Helens.

The first 8ft (2,438mm) wide and 30ft (9,144mm) long bus to operate in Wolverhampton was WUK19, an Arab IV with a one-off flat-fronted style by Burlingham delivered in 1958. Similar vehicles were to follow with lower cost bodies by Metro-Cammell. The advertising for 'Tweedies' was a distinctive feature of this bus that was retained for most of its life in service, which came to an end in 1974. CW

Viewed at the same location in Wolverhampton, YDA38 was one of the batch of Metro-Cammell bodied Arab IVs in the style of WUK19, which can be seen in the background. CW

JOHANNESBURG JUMBOS

During the later years of the 1950s, a batch of ten exceptionally large high-capacity bus chassis was exported by Guy to South Africa; these were fitted with bodies locally by Bus Bodies Ltd based in Port Elizabeth. These were three-axle heavyweight chassis that quickly acquired the name of 'Megadeckers' and were intended for peak-time operation on routes where the expansion of the existing trolleybus system could not be justified. Measuring 34ft (10,363mm) in length and 8ft 6in (2,590mm) wide, they were powered by a 6-cylinder Rolls-Royce C6.NFR 12.17-litre diesel engine specially set for use at the altitude of Johannesburg, developing 156bhp and 425ft lb of torque. At sea level, the standard settings of the engine allowed it to develop 210bhp.

The size of the locally bodied Guy chassis shipped to Johannesburg is apparent in this image. AMRTM/GUY ARCHIVE

Transmission was via a Guy preselective five-speed gearbox with ratios of 5.55:1, 4.2:1, 2.38:1, 1.57:1 and a direct top gear driving through a 6.75:1 ratio back axle. The buses provided seating for eighty-five and room for twenty standing passengers, making them, at the time, the largest double-deckers in service anywhere in the world. Maximum weight, fully laden, was in the region of 19 tons (19,300kg), with air brakes and power-assisted steering.

In addition to the ten diesel-powered 'Megadeckers', the order also included a further forty high-capacity trolleybus chassis that were supplied by Guy's associate company, Sunbeam.

Eleven Park Royal-bodied Arab IV buses were shipped to Kenya for service in Nairobi during 1957. These high-capacity buses had seating for seventy passengers. Number 160 in the fleet is looking a little tired in this photograph en route to Jericho, a suburb to the east of the city.

Twenty-six Roe Arab IVs with low-bridge bodies were taken into stock by the West Riding Automobile Company in 1955, followed by five ultra low-bridge buses the following year and a further batch of forty-five in 1957, one of which is preserved at the Dewsbury Bus Museum. These were amongst the very last sunken gangway low-bridge buses to operate in Great Britain. CW

As the 1950s came to their close, it appeared that the market in the 1960s for traditional front-engined, half-cab vehicles was about to change in favour of the new forward-entrance vehicles, mostly with rear engines. Guy Motors, not wishing to be left behind, had its own thoughts on the future, which will be told in a later chapter.

APRIL 1955 – A GOOD MONTH FOR BUSINESS

Guy Motors were pleased to publish that during April 1955 they had received orders totalling £544,687, with slightly more than half of this being for export. Singapore Traction Company placed an order for forty single-deck Arab buses, União de Transportadores para Importação e Comércio (UTIC) in Portugal ordered twenty-two vehicles, customers in South Africa placed orders for twenty and a further eighteen were to be shipped to East Africa. For home use, Edinburgh Corporation ordered fifty double-deckers, Lancashire United Transport ordered ten, while Middlesbrough Corporation placed an order for eight. Other municipal operators placed smaller orders during the same month, totalling a further twenty-one vehicles. It was a good month for business.

A collection of technical press advertisements placed by Guy Motors promoting the cost savings that could be achieved using Guy's products, and celebrating repeat orders placed for new vehicles.

Chapter 7

UTILITIES REBUILT AND VARIATIONS ON A THEME

The urgent requirement to increase the fleet of buses in the years following World War II created numerous problems for operators and suppliers alike. In the case of the utility bodies, it was very apparent that while the chassis and mechanicals may have been nearly indestructible, this could not be said about the bodies, which were showing signs of damage and decay at an early stage in their life, arising from the use of unseasoned softwood in their framing and not helped in the majority of cases by the use of steel panelling in lieu of the lighter and more corrosion-resistant aluminium sheet. With steel having a mass of approximately double that of aluminium, the additional weight of the steel-clad bodies added to operating costs, while also increasing the occurrence of structural failure. The austere interiors, lack of ventilation from opening windows, and especially the wooden slat seating fitted to the earliest utility buses were not popular with passengers.

From the 500 utility Arabs delivered in 1942–3, around fifty-seven were rebuilt by a variety of coachbuilders, with large numbers of rebuilds being shared between Northern Counties and Charles H. Roe, while Weymann and Eastern Coach Works reconstructed most of the remainder. There is no discernible pattern in the rebuilds, other than specific operators having a preference for certain coachworks, and all builders replaced bodies built by others; the only instance noted of a builder replacing a body that they had originally built was a batch of three supplied to Maidstone and District in 1943 carrying Weymann bodies that were rebuilt in 1952 by Weymann.

The life of these early build utility buses was to be very short, with new bodies being fitted from 1948

Originally delivered in 1941 with a low-bridge body by Duple, EWO467 was rebodied in 1950 by BBW and in 1965 it found its way to Provincial in Fareham, in whose depot it is seen here.

The territory operated by Aldershot & District contained several railway bridges that mandated the use of low-bridge buses, including the three seen here that were delivered as Arab Is fitted with Strachan bodies, all of which were replaced during 1950 with the Weymann bodies seen here. CW

when three vehicles operated by Edinburgh Corporation had their original Pickering bodies replaced with new bodies built by Northern Coachbuilders (not to be confused with Northern Counties). The Pickering bodies had gained a reputation for poor quality even amongst the utility vehicles and this might be accounted for by Pickering of Wishaw having its origins and primary business in constructing wagons and coaches for the railway, where the loading is carried on a substantial frame and not subject to the same stresses as a road vehicle. Similarly, two high-bridge bodied utilities both originally built by Massey were replaced, one operated by Harper of Heath Hayes in the West Midlands during 1948 with a low-bridge body by Burlingham with a reduced seating capacity of fifty-three, and the other operated by Yorkshire Woollen District, which gained a new Brush body in 1949, losing seating for two in the process.

The bulk of the rebuilds took place between 1951–5. Having been rebuilt, many of these vehicles went on to provide long service for their operators; a case in point being a batch supplied with Roe bodies during 1942 to Lancashire United Transport that were rebuilt in 1955,

gaining new, higher capacity Northern Counties bodies with the now rebuilt buses remaining in service until finally withdrawn in 1966, having provided a total of twenty-four years' service.

A very early rebuild of an Arab I occurred in January 1945, when a formerly Park Royal-bodied bus emerged from the Works of Northern Coachbuilders at Cramlington in Northumberland, now the recipient of a new body. Given the fleet number G30 by London Transport when delivered in December 1942, the bus was about eighteen months old and had been in service for a year when in June 1944 it was severely damaged by the explosion of a V1 doodlebug flying bomb. Once rebuilt, it remained in service in the capital until it was withdrawn during the summer of 1952, when, like so many of the other London Transport Guy utilities, it was sold for export and found further long service in Ceylon (now Sri Lanka).

Arab II vehicles were also candidates for early rebuild, with around 400 of the nearly 2,400 chassis gaining new bodies between 1951–60. Charles H. Roe gained substantial business from these rebuilds, with

Midland Red took a fleet of ten Arab Is with Weymann bodies and forty-eight Arab IIs with bodies provided by Northern Counties, Park Royal and Weymann. HHA61 seen here was one of the later batch with a Park Royal body and was rebuilt in 1950 by Brush with a much revised front, now extended to finish flush with the radiator and with the nearside wing lowered. Sliding window ventilators have been installed and the windows are now rubber mounted.

undertakings also commissioned comprehensive rebuilding programmes, with the work being entrusted to Charles H. Roe. Once again, long service was obtained, with, as an example, the Wolverhampton rebuilds surviving to the early 1960s.

Some operators were to rebuild almost their entire fleets of Arab IIs. As an example, Maidstone and District, which had taken delivery of thirty-three Arab IIs in 1943–4, found a need to rebody all but three during the period between 1949–55. The original Maidstone fleet was fitted with a mixture of Park Royal and Weymann bodies, with the rebuilds split between Weymann and Charles H. Roe.

Elsewhere in the south of England, Southampton Corporation Transport, an undertaking that during the 1950s became a committed Guy operator, withdrew the bulk of its fleet of utility buses with their original bodies starting as early as 1950. Another south coast operator that kept most of its utility vehicles as built was Southdown, which had received a fleet of one hundred Arab utility buses, all except for the first two to be delivered to Arab II specification for service across the extensive network. Deliveries had commenced in 1943 and continued for three years. Ninety-four of the vehicles were fitted with high-bridge bodies, construction being shared primarily among Park Royal, Northern Counties and Weymann. Three high-bridge bodies had been supplied by Strachans,

some 117 new bodies being fitted, including a few replacing bodies of their own original construction and being supplied in number to Wolverhampton Corporation, where the entire fleet of Arab IIs was fitted with new bodies. Devon General and the various Yorkshire

Number 22 in North Western Road Car Company's fleet was new in 1944, an Arab II fitted with a low-bridge Roe body that was replaced in 1950 with the new body seen here, built by Willowbrook with distinctive front ventilators in the upper saloon. In this form, the bus remained in service until 1963. CW

but these were to be replaced with bodies by East Lancs Coachbuilders that had been removed from older buses during the 1950s. Construction of the six low-bridge bodies was split evenly between Strachans and Weymann. Many of these vehicles remained in revenue service with Southdown into the late 1950s, with ad hoc repairs and rebuilding as necessary, including changes to seating capacity. Some were eventually sold for scrap, or to other bus operators and contractors for further service prior to final scrapping in the 1960s.

Two examples of the fleet of utility buses converted to open top by Southdown. GUF123, an Arab II, was delivered late in 1944 with a Northern Counties body and powered by a Gardner 6LW engine, while 171 followed a year later with a Park Royal body and powered with a 5LW, which would need to work hard on the indicated journey from Pool Valley coach station to the Devil's Dyke. CW

Southdown converted thirty-three of this fleet to open top. One of them was used as a tree lopper, but the remainder continued in service, providing open-top bus services along the seafront areas serviced by the company and to landmarks such as the Devil's Dyke and Beachy Head, until eventually replaced in 1963–4 by the large influx of convertible Northern Counties-bodied Leyland PD3s, at which time the utility buses were finally

withdrawn. The tree lopper remained in service with the company until it, too, was finally withdrawn from the Bognor Regis depot in the summer of 1969. One of the fleet, registered GUF 191 and given the fleet number 451, was withdrawn by Southdown along with its contemporaries in 1964 and exported to Denmark, where it operated at a tourist railway until 1971. It eventually returned to the UK in 2001 for restoration.

Bournemouth Corporation also converted some of its utility vehicles for open-top seafront services, but chose to cut them down to single deck. cw

Another of the Bournemouth fleet, FRU224, found further use fitted with a crane to assist with the maintenance of poles to support the overhead for the extensive trolleybus network and then as a means of removing and replacing the roofs for the convertible Daimler Fleetline buses that arrived in 1965. cw

Bournemouth's Arab-derived crane gives a demonstration of removing the roof from the town's convertible Fleetlines during a depot open day. CW

East Kent Road Car Company also converted utility buses for seafront service. BJG353 was an Arab II with a Park Royal body new in the summer of 1944 and is seen here now in open-top form travelling east along Marine Drive in Margate and just about to pass another of the open-top fleet. CW

AN EXCHANGE BETWEEN CAPITALS

In some fleets where the Guy vehicles were a relatively small number overall and where later Guy models were not intended to play a part in the plans for future acquisitions, there was a desire to replace them with other vehicles as quickly as possible, especially in situations where the vehicles were unpopular with the crews. A particular example of the latter situation concerned London Transport, where the fleet of Arabs with reverse gear changes was unpopular with crews who were having high expectations set by the introduction of the standard RT type with its air-operated preselect gear change. Although traffic levels in the metropolis were a small fraction of those experienced in current times, the volume of traffic created a difficult working environment for the driver needing to handle a manual crash gearbox in dense City and West End traffic, especially when compared with the relative ease of handling a new RT. The London Transport RT brought with it the well-known advantage of interchangeability, allowing vehicles to be taken in to have body and mechanicals separated, overhauled and returned to service with the original body and chassis not needing to be matched. Clearly, such a scheme can only operate where standardization is established, and the Guy vehicles did not fit into this regime.

Coincidentally, in the early 1950s Edinburgh Corporation had an urgent requirement to obtain additional buses to allow the existing tram system to be converted to motor buses, and the availability of significant numbers of relatively new well-maintained vehicles being available for rebuilding and rebodying was of great interest. To allow this to proceed, Edinburgh Corporation arranged with Guy Motors in late 1951 for sixty of the unwanted London Transport utility buses to be taken in for refurbishment and rebodying. On the surface, it appeared to be an equitable solution, with one capital city having assets that it wished to dispose of and a second capital city having a requirement. In an environment of severe austerity and an overarching emphasis on industry to manufacture for export and so earn essential foreign

currency, it appeared to meet in full all the Government and national objectives of the time.

Neither party to the agreement was therefore prepared for the reaction by the British Transport Commission (BTC), which had ultimate sanction over the publicly owned London Transport, to set about blocking this specific arrangement and any other undertaking operating under its control from selling surplus or otherwise unwanted buses to operators outside the BTC group, for fear of them falling into the ownership of independent operators setting up as competitors to the nationalized undertaking. Perhaps there were fears of a repetition of the situation after World War I, when the disposal of military surplus vehicles created something of a free-for-all in road transport, or perhaps it was a move to stifle competition, but the rule was that BTC companies could only sell assets within the group, for export or for scrap. A plan was quickly hatched whereby the nationalized Scottish Bus Group, which would also be a beneficiary from the expansion of the Scottish capital's bus system, would act as an intermediary in the deal, although in the end common sense prevailed and an arrangement was struck directly between London Transport and Edinburgh Corporation, on the strict understanding that at the end of their lives in the Edinburgh fleet, the vehicles would be scrapped.

Sixty of the withdrawn London Transport Arab II buses fitted with Gardner 5LW engines were selected

The surviving example from the fleet of sixty former London Transport utility Arab buses that were rebuilt for Edinburgh Corporation.

Despite the initial appearance of a flat-fronted bus designed in the style that was becoming fashionable during the 1950s, the Edinburgh rebuilds were fitted with a conventional bonnet covering the engine and the space next to the driver's half-cab was left unglazed.

and purchased in early 1952. The bodies were removed for scrap and the chassis and mechanical items were overhauled to such an extent that a new chassis number was deemed necessary before the refurbished chassis were fitted with new Duple bodies at the premises of Nudd Bros and Lockyer at Kegworth in Leicestershire, with deliveries to Edinburgh starting at the end of 1952 and running into the middle of 1953, when the last of the rebuilds was supplied. With the buses having a new chassis number and a new body, they were deemed to be completely new vehicles and accordingly allocated new, Scottish, registration numbers. To the casual observer or passenger, they appeared to be completely new vehicles.

The lightweight bodies seated fifty-five passengers in total, with thirty-one upstairs and just twenty-four downstairs, including a full-width reverse-facing front seat for five passengers. Entrance was by way of a conventional open rear platform with a straight staircase, resulting in the usual offside transverse seat being replaced with a luggage space. Viewed from the front or nearside, these new bodies created the impression of a flat-fronted vehicle; it was only on closer examination that it could be seen that the nearside front and forward side glazing were missing and a conventional opening bonnet was fitted.

Now in their second lives, the vehicles remained in service in Edinburgh, with withdrawals commencing in 1967 and continuing until 1969. In accordance with the original agreement, all were eventually scrapped, with the exception of one vehicle that has been preserved.

MORE REBUILDS IN SCOTLAND

Further batches of withdrawn London Transport Arab IIs also found their way to Scotland for new lives, but as these were all within the BTC grouping, the issues that came to light with the Edinburgh conversions did not surface. Twenty-three were rebuilt by Scottish Omnibuses, having first been lengthened to take 30ft (9,144mm) length bodies, with seventeen receiving thirty-nine seat front-entrance single-deck bus bodies and six receiving thirty-five seat front-entrance coaches. All were built on frames provided by Walter Alexander and were, like the Edinburgh rebuilds, modified and rebuilt to such an extent that the authorities determined that they should be given new registrations. Finally, a further ten withdrawn London Transport Arab IIs were rebodied in 1954 by Northern Counties, with low-bridge bodies seating fifty-one passengers for Western SMT.

SOUTH COAST REBUILDS

One of the more interesting smaller independent bus operators on the south coast, the Gosport and Fareham Omnibus Company, was a subsidiary of the Provincial Tramways Company. Its base of operations was located at the junction of services provided by the much larger Southdown and Hants & Dorset Motor Services, which both also operated in the town of Fareham, but left the Gosport area to the company that was always known as Provincial, it being the sole surviving operating business of the once extensive Provincial tramways system. While Hants & Dorset and Southdown both operated mostly standardized fleets, with Bristols arriving from Southampton and Winchester for the former, and Leylands from Portsmouth in Southdown colours, the Provincial fleet was one that can only be described as eclectic. It operated a mixture of AECs and Guys of various origins and vintages working short but heavily patronized services in and around Gosport, with many services heading to the passenger ferry terminal to unload workers and service personnel employed in the naval dockyard a short ferry ride across the harbour, or in the many supply depots in Gosport itself. As such, the vehicles were worked hard and sometimes appeared careworn, unlike their Southdown rivals, which were invariably smartly turned out, or the uniform Bristol/ECW combination in standard Tilling livery.

Provincial 55 is an Arab I delivered in late 1942 with a Weymann body that was replaced in 1955 with this new body by Readings, a Portsmouth-based coachbuilder … CW

… while 57 in the fleet is an Arab II originally fitted with a Park Royal body prior to gaining its new convertible body built by Readings in 1953.

Six Arab IIs with Park Royal utility bodies were delivered in 1943, with a further four following two years later; between 1947–54, a number of new vehicles from AEC and Guy, the latter predominately with Park Royal bodies built by Guy, were purchased and from then until 1968, other than two new Guys delivered in 1958, only second-hand vehicles were obtained, including a number of former Southampton Corporation Arabs, also fitted with Park Royal bodies. It was during this later period that a number of interesting and innovative rebuilds took place.

The first of the utility buses to have been delivered, registered EHO228 and given the fleet number of 55, was delivered with a Weymann body that was replaced in 1955 with a locally designed and built body by the firm of Readings, who were established just across the harbour in Portsmouth and had provided a similarly styled body for that city's earlier intake of Leyland PD1s. A similar rebody was performed to EHO869, fleet number 57,

which received a new body in 1953 seating fifty-four passengers and with fitted platform doors, ideal for private hire and known as a 'coach bus'. Unusually, this body was designed to be convertible to open top for summer use, when a set of rails would be fitted. Some difficulties were experienced in removing the roof, with a tendency for the glazing to fall out. Both 55 and 57 have been preserved.

More radical rebodies occurred starting in 1956, when a flat-fronted body, also by Readings, was fitted to two members of the fleet. Although this modernized the frontal appearance of the vehicle, the original distinctive exposed radiator was retained, now contained behind a removable body panel to allow for the coolant level to be checked. This body style was also used on further Arabs that were extensively rebuilt with overhauled chassis and fitted with new engines.

Twelve Arab IIs were substantially rebuilt and re-engined by Gosport & Fareham. Rather than the simple

Originally delivered in 1945 with a Park Royal body and carrying fleet number 17, this is an example of the flat-front rebuild style fitted by Readings. CW

RIGHT: The same bus showing how the false front covered the traditional exposed radiator to give a more modern appearance. The nearside door is labelled as a luggage compartment. CW

approach of replacing the engines with new Gardners, the decision was taken by the Managing Director of the company, H. Orme-White (who had been in charge of day-to-day operations since 1936 and would remain in charge until 1967, when he finally retired at the advanced age of eighty-one), to adopt something more radical. Listening to reports of air-cooled diesel lorries from employees who had served in the Forces in Germany, enquiries were made with the firm of Deutz in Cologne and their model F6L 514 6-cylinder inline engine with a capacity of 7226cc was selected. This provided 125bhp at 2,300rpm, torque of 332ft lb at 1,200rpm, and with an idling speed of 500rpm was faster running and more powerful than the Gardner it was intended to replace.

Between 1957–62, five Arab IIs previously operated by Provincial were converted and fitted with the new flat-front body, with additional heat and sound insulation fitted over the engine compartment. A further seven vehicles were acquired from various sources for conversion from 1962–7. The first five to be converted

883HHO was originally delivered to Yorkshire Woollen as HD7651 before being purchased by Provincial, rebodied with a new flat-front double-deck body by Readings and fitted with a Deutz air-cooled engine. CW

The single-deck bus also started life as a double-deck Arab III with United Welsh prior to it, too, being drastically rebuilt and fitted with an air-cooled engine. Despite its 1967 registration, the original chassis was delivered in 1951. THE OMNIBUS SOCIETY

retained their original registration, but the licensing authorities later determined that the conversions were so radical that it was appropriate for a new registration to be issued. Of the batch of acquired vehicles, all except one were double-deck vehicles to the same style as the earlier rebuilds, the exception being a specially designed single-deck bus with perimeter seating used on a route that entailed crossing a narrow railway bridge. All remained in service into the 1970s, with withdrawals starting in 1970 and the final rebuilt vehicle being withdrawn in 1973. Despite having a distinctive sound, the converted buses were not exceptionally noisy to travel on.

LINCOLN AIR-COOLED GUY

In 1948, Lincoln Corporation purchased a fleet of ten Guy Arab IIIs with the standard Guy bodies built on Park Royal frames, of which fleet number 23 was the first to be completed and was shown on the Guy Motors stand at the Commercial Motor Show that year. The other nine buses in the batch were fitted with Gardner 6LW engines, but this vehicle was powered with the Meadows option. A number of other useful features were fitted, including a warning lamp to indicate to the driver if a passenger was being dragged behind the bus (a feature

that was not a success), and an additional lamp to indicate that a passenger had operated a bell push to indicate a request stop, a feature that has been generally adopted on modern vehicles. The driver was provided with a push switch to reset the indicator. Several engine replacements occurred, including a second Meadows unit and eventually a Leyland 6-cylinder diesel, until the bus was withdrawn from service in 1959 following a failure of this final engine.

The local engineering firm of Ruston & Honsby, a company with a history dating back to the 1840s and with an established reputation for building stationary engines and small railway locomotives, had developed an air-cooled diesel engine from an earlier marine engine that was similar in size and performance to the Deutz units employed in the Provincial conversions and the opportunity was taken to install an example experimentally in number 23. Visually, the new cover replacing the original radiator was the only clue to the modifications. The conversion proved to be successful in service, giving a vehicle with lively performance. It survived until 1967, after which it was saved for preservation. Unlike the Deutz conversions operating in Fareham and Gosport, which were not excessively noisy inside, the Ruston conversion gained a reputation for its noise with reports of conductors struggling to hear passengers stating their destinations when purchasing tickets.

Lincoln Corporation's take on an air-cooled conversion was less drastic than the approach taken by Provincial, with only the revised frontal appearance revealing that this was not a standard Park Royal-bodied Arab III.

Chapter 8

OTTERS, VIXENS, WARRIORS AND VICTORIES

The small and now rather outdated normal-control Guy Wolf was reintroduced in 1946 and remained in production little changed from the pre-war model until 1954, other than a revised radiator grill in keeping with the Arab models. A revised Vixen, designated as LLV, also reappeared in 1946 as a forward-control vehicle built on a 14ft 9in (4,495mm) wheelbase for a body length of about 24ft (7,315mm) and powered initially by a 4-cylinder petrol engine providing 58bhp with transmission by a four-speed constant-mesh gearbox. Braking, in keeping with Guy vehicles of the period, utilized a hydraulic system. For 1948, a new engine option was provided, this being the 4-cylinder Perkins diesel P4, with models so fitted being designated LLVDP.

Then in 1950 a new model suitable for bus or coach bodies seating up to thirty passengers arrived on the market, based on the Vixen, but built with a stronger chassis, fitted with larger wheels and marketed as the Guy Otter. A two-speed rear axle giving ratios of 4.5:1 and 6.25:1, as opposed to the single-speed ratio of 5.625:1, was listed and the sales brochure boasted a top speed of 50mph (80km/h). Power was again from a 4-cylinder petrol engine or from a Gardner 4LK 4-cylinder diesel of 3800cc capacity. With this engine, a fuel economy of 19–24mpg (15–11.8ltr/100km) could be achieved, at least if the brochure can be believed. An additional engine option was added in 1952, again from Perkins, but this time a 6-cylinder P6.

From the late 1940s the market for twenty-five to thirty seat small coaches was dominated by the Bedford OB/Duple Vista combination. Guy's Wolf, Vixen and Otter joined Bedford in competing for market share.

This brochure image shows the general assembly for the Vixen chassis.

New to Court Cars of Torquay in 1948 was this Guy Vixen equipped with a twenty-nine seat coach body constructed by Wadhams. Seen here at the Black Country Living Museum in Dudley. TONY HISGETT

Guy's sales material for their range of smaller bus and coach chassis included this illustration of a Vixen fitted with a body similar to that seen in the previous image.

The Channel Islands are located between England and France. Guernsey, the smaller of the two major islands, has severe restrictions on vehicle dimensions dictated by the size of the roads, which made this Duple-bodied Vixen ideal for use as a bus, seen here at Town Terminus in St Peter Port.

Guy's *Light Passenger Chassis* brochure also included this illustration of the chassis for the Otter.

Originally built in 1950 as a Guy demonstrator and fitted with a twenty-nine seat forward-entrance coach body by Alexander, NTB403 went into service with bus and coach operator Hulley's. It is photographed here in preservation.

LONDON TRANSPORT'S GUY SPECIAL

At the beginning of the 1950s, London Transport established a requirement for a fleet of small single-deck buses to serve the country routes outside the metropolitan area. Although some of the routes provided sufficient loading to justify double-deck or large-capacity single-deck buses, many served sparsely populated areas or covered narrow country roads where a full-size vehicle was not a practical proposition. These were being serviced by a fleet of Leyland Cubs, most of which were reaching the end of their lives, and a newer, rear-engined version of the Cub built by Leyland and designated CR by London Transport. A better solution was required. The large new single-deck RF then under development would be used on many country routes, but was still deemed too large for certain routes that required a vehicle of about twenty-four seats that would be ideally suited to one-man operation.

The ideal solution was a more modern version of something like the earlier Cub, probably normal-control, diesel-engined and available without long delivery times. With all the established London Transport suppliers working to full capacity with new builds and refurbishment of wartime utility vehicles, this posed something of a dilemma. London Transport determined that it would need a

GS42 is a perfectly restored and preserved example of the London Transport country area Guy Special, seen here at a classic vehicle rally in the summer of 2017.

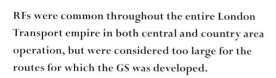

RFs were common throughout the entire London Transport empire in both central and country area operation, but were considered too large for the routes for which the GS was developed.

fleet of eighty-four vehicles. The solution was something of a 'parts bin special', using a Guy Motors chassis clothed with a body by Eastern Coach Works to a design specified by London Transport and finished with a front assembly produced by Briggs Motor Bodies; this was in the same style with minor changes as was being pressed for use in Ford Motor Company's medium-weight Thames lorries and Leyland's similar sized Comets.

The chassis was a slightly modified Vixen chassis, powered by a derated Perkins P6 6-cylinder diesel engine with transmission via a four-speed constant-mesh gearbox normally fitted to the Vixen and lever operated, with the change lever located conventionally to the left of the driver's seat but arranged in the reversed H pattern. Guy gave this chassis the designation NLLVP.

The Eastern Coach Works body featured many design elements from the RF and when viewed from the rear, the similarity is quite obvious, as is the internal finish. One notable difference is the use of sliding ventilators in the windows, rather than the wind-down drop lights that remained a feature of other London buses for many years into the future. Seating twenty-six passengers, special dispensation was sought and obtained for the buses to be operated as driver-only vehicles; the economics of many of the routes where they operated would have rendered crew operation uneconomic. London Transport gave the new bus the designation of 'Guy Special', or GS.

The first sixty-six GS buses entered service between October 1953 and January 1954, with distribution around the country area depots, where they were put into service as planned. The expansion of new towns around London resulted in green London Transport buses reaching as far as Harlow in Essex, Hemel Hempstead and Stevenage, both in the county of Hertfordshire, and Crawley in West Sussex, although in many cases the population growth soon justified the operation of larger capacity vehicles.

Most of the GS fleet lasted into the 1960s, although the introduction in 1962 of the coach-seated Routemasters on to the longer distance country area routes resulted in a cascade of earlier RFs, which were now permitted to be operated solely by the driver, to replace the GS; this was to result in some being placed into storage and others being sold out of service to new owners. The remaining fleet continued to operate the routes that could not handle the larger vehicles, as peak service supplemental

Viewed from the rear, the GS shared a similar appearance to the RF, despite being built by different coachbuilders.

capacity and for use as staff buses, with some reintroduced on their original routes where a drop in patronage made the RFs uneconomic. Reorganization in 1970 saw the country area bus operations renamed as London Country, with the final public service operated by a GS being in March 1972 in and around the Rickmansworth area in the leafy outer north-western suburbs.

It was usual practice for London Transport to remove all manufacturer's identification from its vehicles, but not in the case of the GS vehicles, where the familiar Guy 'Feathers in our Cap' emblem was shown above the London Transport Logo.

GUY VIXEN-BASED SPECIAL PASSENGER CHASSIS FOR LONDON TRANSPORT SPECIFICATION

Layout

Normal-control four-wheel front engine chassis for single-deck bodywork

Engine — Perkins P6

Bore and stroke — Bore: 3.5in (88.9mm), stroke: 5in (127mm)

Capacity — 4.73 litres

Valves — 2 valves per cylinder

Power — 65bhp at 2,200rpm

Transmission

Clutch — Friction clutch, single plate

Gearbox — Four-speed, constant mesh

Overall ratios:

1st — 5.5:1

2nd — 3.15:1

3rd — 1.7:1

4th — 1:1

Reverse — 6.6:1

Suspension and steering

Suspension — Semi-elliptic front and rear, hydraulic shock absorbers

Steering — Marles cam and double roller steering box

Axles

Front — I section

Rear — Ratio 5.7:1

Electrical system — 24V system, electrically operated passenger door

Brakes

Type — Foot brake operating drums on all wheels; vacuum-assisted employing Lockheed Hydrovac Front drums 16.5in diameter × 4in wide (419 × 102mm) Rear drums 16.25 diameter × 6.5in wide (412.75 × 165mm)

Handbrake — Conventional lever, operating on rear wheels only

Dimensions (including body)

Overall length — 25ft (7,620mm)

Overall width — 7ft 6in (2,286mm)

Wheelbase — 15ft (4,572mm)

Unladen weight — 4 tons (4,064kg)

Fuel tank capacity — 17.5gal (79.5ltr)

The fleet of Mulliner-bodied Guys operated in the Isle of Man had a similar appearance to the more numerous GS examples. Fleet number 9 is preserved and is seen here inside the Transport Museum at Wythall.

The very large destination screens fitted to the Mulliner-bodied Guys operated in the Isle of Man probably added nothing to the aerodynamic qualities of these vehicles.

A small additional batch of five chassis designated NLLODP was built in 1957 for Douglas Corporation, fitted with bodies that were generally similar to the Eastern Coach Works bodies, but built by Mulliners and with a distinctively large front destination screen. They were to operate on the Isle of Man until 1970.

New Owners

Tillingbourne Bus Company had taken over a series of former London Transport routes in the Guildford area in Surrey and acquired eight GS buses to serve many of the same routes that it had previously operated for London Transport. Further south, Southern Motorways, an operating company within the web of businesses operated by Basil Williams, had obtained a number of GS buses to operate services in the area north and west of Chichester in West Sussex. Two went to West Bromwich Corporation, where one was modified for use as transport for the local Social Services Department, while many examples were bought for private bus use by contractors and agricultural workers. Some later became mobile homes and many have ultimately found their way into preservation where they remain an attractive proposition as a cherished vehicle by virtue of their size and public affection.

Formerly GS76 and one of the vehicles that was purchased by Tillingbourne, MXX376 continues the type of service for which it was designed in Surrey. CW

ABOVE: **GS81 was withdrawn and sold in 1964, finding further use as a community transport vehicle with the Assemblies of God Church in Bromley, Kent. It is seen here in Masons Hill in the town.** CW

Two examples of GSs that were sold to Basil Williams' Southern Motorways business, where they provided a service between the town of Emsworth and the former RAF station at Thorney Island, a distance of less than 3 miles. Some of these remained in service until the mid-1970s, by which time they were in poor condition. CW

HENRY MEADOWS LIMITED

The output of Henry Meadows Ltd occurs regularly in the chronology of the products of Guy Motors. The company was first established in April 1919 with an intention to manufacture proprietary gearboxes for supply to the burgeoning number of vehicle manufacturers. A factory was soon established at Park Lane, Wolverhampton, conveniently close to Guy's Fallings Park Works. The first product was supplied in 1920 to the Vulcan Motor and Engineering Company, providing three forward and one reverse speed. The first internal combustion engine was to follow in time for the 1922 London Motor Show, then held at the exhibition centre in Olympia. This was a 4-cylinder ohv petrol engine of 1.25 litres capacity and built in small numbers, with production of around eight completed engines weekly. Meadows established themselves as a valued supplier of petrol engines to many of the growing car builders in the 1920s, including Lagonda and Invicta, for whom a 4.5-litre 6-cylinder engine was supplied, while the smaller 4-cylinder engines found a ready market with the smaller manufacturers now established in the Midlands.

Henry Meadows died in July 1937 at the young age of fifty-seven, but the company to which he had given his name continued and became a valuable supplier to Guy Motors, who were a major customer for the Meadows 4 ELA engine, used in both passenger and goods vehicles, while with the coming of World War II, Meadows were to develop suitable engines to power tanks, including a 12-cylinder, horizontally opposed engine for the new Cruiser tank.

Development on compression ignition engines had commenced in the 1930s, leading to the series of 'square' engines with 5.11in (130mm) bore and stroke built as both 4- and 6-cylinder units for vertical and horizontal installation and, again, offered as options by Guy Motors. Important features of the Meadows design were the compactness of the engine, the ability to mount ancillaries on either side of the block (especially useful to operators of half-cab buses fitted with left-hand drive) and the relatively high output for the capacity. As well as for use in underfloor-engined buses, the horizontal engines, especially those of larger capacity, also found application on the railways, where they provided power to railcars. This was to lead to a business relationship with Brush Engineering that resulted in Meadows building large diesel engines for use in railway locomotives. Unfortunately, in use, they developed a reputation in some quarters for fragility, especially relating to failures of crankshafts. Meadows developed a range of electrical generating sets, powered by their own engines, that were to prove to be both rugged and reliable; perhaps the constant running speed suited them better. Henry Meadows Ltd became part of Associated British Engineering Ltd in 1952 and on 1 January 1965 was acquired by Jaguar Cars.

WARRIOR AND WARRIOR LUF

The tough operating conditions of the East and South African countries where Guy had a well-developed market required a robust vehicle, which resulted in Guy developing the Warrior model in 1956 – a front-engined model that would cope with rutted surfaces and gravel roads. Given the same name as the rugged lorry from the same period, the Warrior was intended to carry bodywork with seating for forty or forty-two passengers and could be supplied with a choice of four different diesel engines and various transmission options, including a two-speed rear axle, the choice of which would be determined by customer preference and the intended application. The chassis layout followed that of the traditional Arab bus chassis and was suitable for centre or rear entrance, although a number of chassis were built in 1958 with the front axle set back to provide for a forward entrance directly opposite the driver for the fitting of a high-capacity urban bus body of the type often known as a trambus.

The features of the Warrior were then developed into an underfloor-engined version, which, following the precedent set with the earlier Arab UF, was naturally given the name of Warrior LUF. Although the Arab UF and LUF had sold in respectable numbers and the Warrior sold well in overseas markets, neither the vertically engined or underfloor-powered Warrior sold well in the domestic market. In 1956, Guy built a Warrior LUF powered by a Meadows 4HDC330 4-cylinder horizontal engine and five-speed gearbox as a demonstrator, first shown at the Commercial Motor Show in September of that year.

This was fitted with a forty-one seat Burlingham Seagull body and other than the underfloor location of the engine and necessary revisions to the chassis layout, the general specification followed that of the traditionally built model. The key chassis dimensions were a wheelbase of 16ft 4in (4,979mm), an overall chassis length of 25ft 2in (7,680mm) and a front overhang of 5ft 1.375in (1,254mm). In addition to the Meadows engine, both the

The **GUY WARRIOR**
VERTICAL ENGINED PASSENGER CHASSIS

GUY MOTORS LTD. **WOLVERHAMPTON**
ALSO AT LONDON · CAPE TOWN · DURBAN · JOHANNESBURG

For a company that had been a pioneer of the underfloor-engined bus and coach chassis, the front vertically engined Warrior may have been seen as a retrograde step, but the increased ground clearance was of benefit to operators, especially in Commonwealth countries. The front-engined format continued to be popular in the light- and middle-weight sector, especially for coaches where Bedford would remain with the format for many years.

AEC AH470 6-cylinder engine and Gardner 5HLW were listed as options. In the case of the AEC engine, the five-speed gearbox provided for a direct top gear, while for the Gardner, the fifth speed was overdriven.

AEC, like Gardner, had a long-established reputation for producing reliable diesel engines, many of which were used in their own build of lorries and buses, not least in London, where they provided power to the vast majority of London Transport's fleet. It was perhaps unfortunate for Guy that the 470 series was one that quickly gained a reputation for being troublesome, with cylinder head gasket failures being common and changes to gasket materials improving, but not fully rectifying, the situation until a revision to the head stud design improved matters.

Commercial Motor took the demonstrator for a road test and published a report in February 1957 which emphasized a number of the key features of the coach, including its low weight (3.5 tons [3,556kg] for the bare chassis and just over 6 tons [6,096kg] with body and fuel) and twin circuit air braking, providing braking to be maintained even if one of the systems should fail; a new feature that had been demonstrated at the Commercial Motor Show the previous year. Loaded with sandbags to give a representative load, the total weight of the vehicle as tested was just short of 9.5 tons (9,652kg); it was found that cruising at the maximum speed of 56mph (90km/h) was possible and at a lower cruising speed of around 30mph (48km/h), a fuel consumption of between 21.6–17.8mpg (13–15.9ltr/100km) was achieved – a remarkable economy. The conclusion for performance and economy was that the complete coach was perfectly suited for long-distance Continental touring. The only negative point in the review concerned the

A seventy-seat Guy Warrior J-type is seen here on the Trans-Nile Express in Uganda, which ran between the capital Kampala and Moyo, a route that covered over 300 miles (480km). The high ground clearance can be seen, as can the capacity to carry large volumes of luggage.

GUY WARRIOR FRONT-ENGINED CHASSIS SPECIFICATION

Layout — Normal-control four-wheel front engine chassis for single-deck bodywork

Engine — Meadows 4DC330, 4-cylinder
Bore and stroke — Bore: 4.72 in (120mm), stroke 4.72in (120mm)
Capacity — 5.43 litres
Power — 85bhp at 2,200rpm
Torque — 230ft lb at 1,350rpm

Transmission
Clutch — Friction clutch, 13in (330mm) single plate
Gearbox — Five-speed, constant mesh
 Overall ratios:
 1st — 6.12:1
 2nd — 3.37:1
 3rd — 1.55:1
 4th — 1:1
 5th — 0.76:1
 Reverse — 5.72:1

Engine — Gardner 4LW, 4-cylinder
Bore and stroke — Bore: 4.25in (108mm), stroke: 6in (152.4mm)
Capacity — 5.6 litres
Power — 75bhp at 1,700rpm
Torque — 237ft lb at 1,300rpm

Transmission — As chassis fitted with Meadows 4DC330

Engine — Leyland 0.350, 6-cylinder
Bore and stroke — Bore: 4in (101.6mm), stroke: 4.75in (120.7mm)
Capacity — 5.76 litres
Power — 100bhp at 2,200rpm
Torque — 255ft lb at 1,400rpm

Transmission
Clutch — Friction clutch, 13in (330mm) single plate
Gearbox — Five-speed, constant mesh
 Overall ratios:
 1st — 7.08:1
 2nd — 4.36:1
 3rd — 2.715:1
 4th — 1.63:1
 5th — 1:1
 Reverse — 6.28:1

Engine — AEC AV470, 6-cylinder
Bore and stroke — Bore: 4.4in (112mm), stroke: 5.11in (130mm)
Capacity — 7.685 litres
Power — 112bhp at 2,000rpm
Torque — 255ft lb at 1,100rpm

Transmission
Clutch — Friction clutch, 13in (330mm) single plate
Gearbox — Five-speed, constant mesh
 Overall ratios:
 1st — 6.25:1
 2nd — 4.4:1
 3rd — 2.65:1
 4th — 1.56:1
 5th — 1:1
 Reverse — 6.01:1

Suspension and steering
Suspension — Semi-elliptic front and rear, hydraulic shock absorbers fitted to front
Steering — Marles cam and double roller steering box

Axles
Front — I section
Rear — Heavy duty Eaton twin speed with a range of ratios available

Electrical system — 24V system, 94AH batteries

Brakes
Type — Foot brake operating drums on all wheels. Bendix-Westinghouse air – hydraulic system. Front drums 15.5in diameter × 4.5in wide (364 × 114mm) Rear drums 15.25 diameter × 6in wide (387 × 152mm)
Handbrake — Conventional lever, operating on rear wheels only

Seen at the Guy factory, this Works image of a Warrior LUF chassis shows the flat run of the main chassis rails, unlike the Arab UF design, which required a raised section over the engine. AMRTM/GUY ARCHIVE

The Commercial Motor Show Guy Warrior with its Burlingham Seagull forty-one seat coach body and later used by Guy Motors as a demonstrator. AMRTM/GUY ARCHIVE

forward entrance, which was mentioned as being narrow and with steep steps as a result of the forward-hinged, inwardly opening door, something that might present difficulties for elderly or infirm passengers. From the driver's perspective, it was noted that the coach was very quiet in operation, making it necessary to keep a constant watch on the speedometer to avoid infringing the 30mph (48km/h) speed limit where it applied.

The Seagull-bodied demonstrator was purchased by Dodds of Troon, who, at the time of publication, still own the vehicle and where it remains in service for special occasions.

For the 1958 Commercial Motor Show, this Warrior with a highly stylish forty-one seat luxury coach body by Mulliner was displayed, powered by a Meadows 4HDC.330 engine. Of particular note are the large glazed areas to the front and rear of the roof. The coach was operated by Castle Coaches of Birmingham. AMRTM/GUY ARCHIVE

Also built in 1958, this Warrior is fitted with a forty-four seat forward-entrance bus body and was initially used as a demonstrator by Guy Motors.

SEAL – ANOTHER UNDERFLOOR DESIGN

With the move towards underfloor-engined buses and coaches, it was inevitable that thoughts would turn to creating an underfloor-engined mid-range chassis to supplement the Otter and Vixen range. The market for this model was clearly identified as Guy's European customers, with the sales brochure cover showing a left-hand drive tourist coach with a Portuguese registration. The Seal was described as a 'single-deck underfloor engined chassis ... designed to meet the requirement of

The Guy Seal was marketed towards Continental operators, with the illustration on the sales material showing a Portuguese registered left-hand drive coach.

operators needing a vehicle suitable for feeder services or a small capacity tourist coach with a high performance'.

Power for the Seal was provided by a Perkins 6-cylinder horizontal engine of 5 litres capacity with a bore of 3.6in (91.4mm) and stroke of 5in (127mm), developing 87bhp at 2,400rpm and delivered through an 11in (280mm) single dry plate clutch to a five-speed constant-mesh David Brown gearbox, with top gear being 22 per cent overdriven. Braking followed the format of the earlier chassis with Hydrovac-assisted hydraulic braking. Two overall chassis lengths were listed: a 21ft (6,400mm) length with 11ft 6in (3,505mm) wheelbase; and a 26ft length (7,925mm) with 14ft 2in (4,318mm) wheelbase.

A VICTORY FOR GUY

1958 saw the announcement of a new Guy product aimed clearly at the luxury long-distance export coach market and containing options that would feature in the forthcoming Wulfrunian double-decker described fully in the following chapter. With an 18ft (5,486mm) wheelbase suitable for bodywork of up to 36ft (10,973mm) in length, it quickly found customers in Holland and Belgium. The first public viewing of the Victory chassis

was at the Dutch Commercial Show held in Amsterdam, where a chassis fitted with an 8-litre Meadows 6HDC500 providing a power output of 150bhp was displayed. Responding to potential customer feedback, Guy also offered a Gardner-powered option, utilizing the established 6HLW with a rating of 112bhp. To accommodate the power difference, revisions were also made to the ratios in the transmission, with options also offered for rear axle ratios. Transmission was provided using a Meadows five-speed gearbox with either a direct or overdriven top gear and with the option of synchromesh or a five-speed semi-automatic epicyclic with fluid flywheel.

A third alternative engine offered was the Leyland UE680, the underfloor version of the O.680 6-cylinder engine providing 150bhp from its 11.1-litre capacity. The 680 was itself an evolution of the long-established O.600 Leyland engine and enjoyed a reputation with commercial vehicle operators on a par with the products from Gardner. One such example was built for operation in Holland and shown at that country's Commercial Show in 1959. This included a ZF 655 six-speed air-assisted synchromesh gearbox with an overdriven top gear of 0.63:1 giving a claimed maximum speed of 75mph (120km/h).

Braking on the Victory chassis was provided using a Bendix-Westinghouse full air split system to drums all

Predating the changes in UK legislation that would permit longer single-deck buses and coaches, the Victory was targeted at the European market and particularly for long-distance holiday services. The cover of the sales leaflet showed a left-hand drive chassis fitted with a luxury touring coach body.

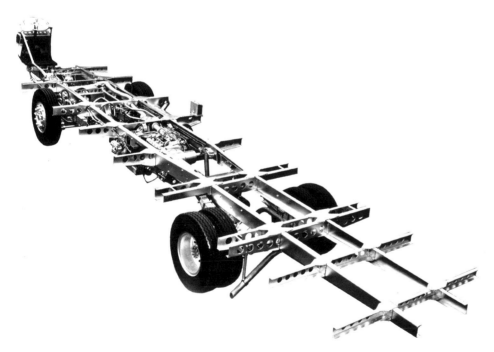

This factory image of the Victory chassis shows the simple but robust style of construction.
AMRTM/GUY ARCHIVE

round, with a mechanical handbrake to the rear wheels and suspension utilized semi-elliptic springs front and rear, with hydraulic lever-type dampers fitted to the front. For the ease of the driver, the clutch and accelerator were both hydraulically operated, although steering using the usual Guy cam and double roller system was not power-assisted. With a fuel tank capacity of 38gal (173ltr) and a typical touring economy of around 12mpg (23.6ltr/100km), a range of 450 miles (725km) could be expected.

A Guy Victory fitted with a Van Hool sixty-one seat coach body was delivered to the firm of DeSwaef, trading as Selecta Cars in Ghent, Belgium, a company that is still in business providing coach hire. It is seen here photographed outside the local agent for Guy Motors. AMRTM/GUY ARCHIVE

Another Benelux delivery was to Franky Tours, also operating in Belgium. Originally delivered with coachwork built locally by Jonckheere, the vehicle was rebuilt with a new body by Van Hool following accident damage. AMRTM/GUY ARCHIVE

AIR SUSPENSION AND DISC BRAKES

An interesting development announced with the Victory chassis was the option of air suspension and disc braking. With the Victory being intended for long-distance Continental touring, thoughts had moved to providing a more comfortable ride over long distances.

In the United States, where even longer distances were frequently covered, self-levelling air suspension had proved to be an attractive method by which to improve passenger comfort and reduce maintenance costs from damaged steel suspension components, as well as reducing general wear and stress-induced damage to bodywork.

The original Victory brochure was recoloured and printed with additional wording to promote the new options of air suspension and disc braking.

Inside the brochure, the chassis photograph emphasized the disc brakes and air suspension system.

In conjunction with air suspension, thoughts were also being given to the adoption of disc braking. Now almost universally fitted, in the late 1950s disc brakes were slowly being introduced to passenger cars, having proved their value first in motor sport. Often thought of as providing more effective braking performance, the real benefit of disc braking in commercial vehicles is the dramatic reduction in brake fade resulting from over-heating friction materials. The system fitted to the air-suspension Victory used an air-pressure boosted hydraulic system, which along with the all-round independent suspension system had similarities in the double-deck stage carriage chassis that was to follow. The application of both air suspension and disc braking was well suited to long-distance operations with limited stops, but as will be seen in the following chapter this was not to be the case when employed on bus services.

VICTORY TRAMBUS

To deal with environments in Commonwealth countries where higher ground clearance was mandated, the Victory chassis was modified to offer a vertically mounted engine located at the front of the vehicle, with a set-back front axle to provide a forward entrance in the

The Victory Trambus was announced as being designed and tested specially for overseas conditions, with maximum capacity on two axles. A special brochure was produced to promote sales.

trambus style. Power came from the newly announced Gardner 6LX 6-cylinder engine, an enlarged and more powerful version of the well-established 6LW, now with a capacity of 10.45 litres and providing 150bhp, still at the low governed speed of 1,700rpm. The standard gearbox fitted was four-speed semi-automatic, with two five-speed options providing either a close range set of gears with a direct top gear, or for longer distance applications, an overdrive top. Additionally, the six-speed ZF synchro-mesh gearbox with air-assisted change was also listed as an option. In other respects, the trambus specification was similar to the underfloor model.

Demonstrating Guy's continuing flexibility to meet customer requirements, an order for South African Railways was fulfilled in 1960 for ten trambus-style vehicles fitted with a Rolls-Royce B81 8-cylinder in-line petrol engine with a capacity of 6.5 litres of a type more usually used in military vehicles. Power was delivered using the ZF six-speed gearbox and the vehicles were completed in South Africa with 35ft length (10,668mm) semi-luxury bodywork. Six further vehicles were also ordered, again with Rolls-Royce petrol engines, but in this case B60 6-cylinder versions.

Chapter 9

WULFRUNIAN – TOO MUCH TOO SOON?

During the 1950s the gradual increase in private car ownership and the growing amount of disposable income began to put pressure on public transport and especially on urban bus services. Although legislation to permit driver-only operation, especially on large-capacity double-deckers was many years hence, some thought was beginning to be given on how this could best be achieved, once the law permitted it. The traditional design of front-engined, rear-entrance vehicle was clearly unsuitable, but the conventional front-engined, front entrance could work, even if it was difficult for the driver to be continually swivelling in his seat while fares were being collected. Placing the entrance door opposite the driver ahead of the front wheels would make operations much easier, in the style that had become popular for underfloor-engined coaches, but while a high floor required on coaches even with horizontal engines was acceptable for long-distance stage carriage services or touring coaches, it was less practical for intensively used urban buses for reasons of quick access, and difficult, if not impossible, to adopt for double-deck vehicles, since the interior headroom would be severely compromised for the vehicle to remain within the height regulations.

An alternative solution, as in the AEC Q-type, positioned the engine longitudinally behind the driver, with the thought that in the case of double-decked vehicles, the staircase could be constructed over the engine. This created potential problems of both cooling and access.

An early attempt to reposition the engine other than alongside the driver was AEC's Q-type built for London Transport in the early 1930s, with the engine positioned behind the driver.

Leyland Motors had been experimenting with new designs throughout the 1950s, initially with a rear engine and rear-entrance design, but quickly progressing to a front entrance, but with the engine contained within the passenger compartment at the rear, making noise levels inside unacceptable.

THE REAR-ENGINE SOLUTION

The solution, therefore, was to place the engine at the rear of the vehicle, outside of the passenger space, with the gearbox alongside and the drive taken forward to the rear axle by means of a short propshaft. An amendment to the Construction and Use Regulations for Public Service Vehicles in 1956 permitted the construction of two-axle double-deck buses to a new maximum length of 30ft (9,144mm), allowing the driving position and entrance to be positioned ahead of the front axle, thereby permitting the driver to supervise passenger loading and in due course as and when the regulations would permit, to collect the fares.

Leyland's final design after several prototypes was launched at the 1958 Commercial Motor Show with the model name of Atlantean, a name in keeping with their theme of double-decker chassis being named after undersea dynasties and following on from the Titan models of conventional design that were to continue in production for many years. A consequence of the design was that the Atlantean offered a low floor and single-step entrance from the kerbside, with just a single internal step-up midway along the lower deck to clear the rear axle. Engine position and location aside, the chassis was otherwise of conventional channel section construction and leaf springs. Power came from the well-proven Leyland O.600 6-cylinder diesel engine, extensively used in earlier bus, coach and heavy haulage products, and transmission was via a pneumo-cyclic semi-automatic gearbox and fluid flywheel, although very early examples incorporated a centrifugal clutch.

Despite the generally cautious and conservative nature of many transport operators, the Atlantean met with great success, with Leyland's order book overwhelmed and deliveries running into several years. Daimler launched a similar product, the Fleetline, in 1960, but fitted with a drop-centre rear axle, allowing for a fully flat floor and easier construction of low-bridge coachwork. The Daimler was powered by either a Gardner 6LW or 6LX engine.

Leyland's Atlantean, especially those fitted with the body of this style by Metro-Cammell, quickly set the style for double-deck buses with its rear engine and front entrance. It is a design that has hardly changed in over sixty years.

A NOVEL APPROACH TO LOW BRIDGES

Low bridges have always presented a challenge to double-deckers, with the conventional solution being the 'low-bridge bus', provided with a reduction in overall height. Although the objective of allowing the vehicle to pass under low bridges could be achieved, it was not without some inconvenience to passengers, who were required to adopt a four-across seating arrangement with a narrow gangway on the upper deck, which downstairs passengers needed to be very careful to avoid with their heads when arising from offside seats, as the upstairs gangway protruded severely into the lower deck headroom.

The Lodekka design from Bristol introduced in 1954 overcame these problems, while being of otherwise conventional construction with front engine, half-cab design and drop-centre rear axle. However, it was only available for sale to the nationalized Tilling group of operators. Other operators looked for alternative solutions. Dennis offered the Loline, a licence-built version of the Bristol, and AEC had the Bridgemaster in their catalogue, but for many the solution remained unchanged, that of the conventional chassis and low-bridge body with all its shortcomings.

The Wakefield area of Yorkshire was served by the West Riding Automobile Company, which was in the late 1950s becoming one of the largest independent bus service operators. Its operating territory included numerous low bridges, high passenger loadings and poor road surfaces and in its employ was Ronald Brookes as Fleet Engineer. Brookes had developed a series of ideas to overcome the issues that he was meeting daily in an effort to keep his fleet in service, with the high loadings and poor road surfaces resulting in frequent broken springs and high wear rates of components such as kingpins. With a degree of serendipity, Guy Motors were also considering future designs to replace the venerable Arab series. The experiments of Leyland with their revolutionary Atlantean would have been known and no doubt the similar work by Daimler would have been of interest. The Birmingham and Midland Motor Omnibus Company (BMMO), better known under its trading name of Midland Red, operated an extensive network in the Midlands including Wolverhampton. It had a reputation for advanced design and construction, remaining one of the few operators to continue to build and operate its own designs. It had already incorporated experimental disc braking and independent suspension as the future for the bus. All of these would have been considerations for the design that would replace the Arab.

In the traditional low-bridge bus, passengers on the upper deck were inconvenienced with four-abreast seating, but on the lower deck the sunken gangway required to provide adequate headroom upstairs impinged into the space above the offside seats, frequently resulting in sore heads for passengers less familiar with the vehicles. In the case of this Duple bodied Arab III operated by Red & White, a luggage rack on the nearside at least equalizes the risk.

Dennis's Loline was a licence-built version of Bristol's Lodekka design that was available in the general market. Use of a lowered chassis frame and a drop-centre axle reduced the height sufficiently to allow seating with a centre aisle on the upper deck and still allow passage under low bridges.

Midland Red was an operator that designed and built its own vehicles, frequently leading the industry with the technology employed. Early examples of the D9 were fitted with disc brakes, but problems of high wear and overheating were seen in service and later builds reverted to drum systems.

A WARNING FROM THE RAILWAY

Steam locomotion power in Great Britain had advanced immeasurably from the 1829 Rainhill trials when *Rocket*, designed by Robert Stephenson, set out the basic layout for steam-powered railway locomotives. Other than a few adventurous designs, improvements until the end of steam power were a matter of carefully considered evolution rather than dramatic revolution. Steam pressure was gradually increased, as materials, science and construction methods improved, reaching a general limit of around 220psi working pressure during the 1930s. Access to boiler ancillaries was made easy by mounting these on the outside of the locomotive, more so on US and European designs, and externally mounted gearing was nearly universal, other than on the Great Western Railway, which had continued with its practice of arranging the gear between the frames. Overall, this created the general appearance and design for the British railway steam locomotive from the 1930s until construction for the mainline ended in 1960.

On the Southern Railway, things were to be a little different. The smallest of the 'Big Four' companies created in 1923, it relied more on passenger traffic than the other grouped companies, so much so that despite serving the smallest geographical area, it carried in excess of a quarter of all passenger journeys and had been an early adopter of electrification. Freight, including that to and from the major port of Southampton, remained steam hauled, as did its long-distance lines, including those to the holiday resorts in Dorset, Devon and Cornwall and to the Kent coast ports for Continental traffic.

In 1937, the Southern's Chief Mechanical Engineer, R.E.L. Maunsell, retired and was replaced by O.V.S. Bulleid. Bulleid had spent his entire career in the railway industry, commencing as an apprentice with the Great Northern Railway in Doncaster and ultimately rising to be assistant to Sir Nigel Gresley prior to coming to the Southern; a move from a company whose designs were at the zenith of the technology to another where electrification was the order of the day and steam was very much in second place. Bulleid was determined to make his mark immediately, with improvements to his predecessor's designs and his work on passenger carriages where his ideas would be carried forward to be integrated much later into the standard carriages of British Railways following nationalization in 1948.

But it was for his revolutionary locomotive designs that Bulleid was to gain fame, or notoriety depending upon viewpoint. In 1938, approval was given to commence on the design of a class of 'Pacific' locomotives that incorporated a number of new and then untried ideas. Great use was made in the construction of the boiler and firebox of welding instead of the traditional riveting. Thermic syphons were also used, dramatically increasing the steam-raising capabilities of the boiler, which was rated at 280psi. The valve gear design incorporated a chain drive, encased in an oil bath located under the boiler and between the frames, following the idea of an internal combustion engine where the moving parts are as far as

Bulleid's locomotives for the Southern Railway were a warning against the implementation of too many new ideas into a new design without adequate time being taken to develop each idea prior to volume construction. When working well, the locos were the match of anything ever built in Britain but most were eventually rebuilt by British Railways. Seen here, *City of Wells*, one of the smaller 'West Country' locos, heads its train away from Corfe Castle in Dorset.

continued overleaf

A WARNING FROM THE RAILWAY *(Continued)*

possible enclosed and force-lubricated. In principle, this would reduce maintenance by ensuring that the valve operating gear was kept lubricated and protected from dirt and ash finding its way into the bearings and causing premature wear. Externally, the locomotives were distinguished by rectangular casing, giving a modern, streamlined appearance that was carried back to the tender, with high side sheets aligning with the carriages behind. Rather than use traditional spoked wheels, a new design of cast wheels was employed, named for their designer and manufacturer: Bulleid-Firth-Brown. The first locomotive was finished in 1941, during the darkest period of World War II, but despite the difficulties of the period an entire class of thirty locomotives was constructed, named ultimately after the shipping lines that used the major ports served by the Southern Railway and thus forming the 'Merchant Navy' class.

Problems arose quickly. The casing for the gear system made setting the valve timing difficult and the casing itself leaked, resulting in a voracious thirst for lubricating oil. The oil that was lost would either fall to the track, causing the engines to slip when starting, or more unfortunately spray over the boiler insulation and create a fire hazard. The tender side sheets created difficulties in filling the tender water tanks, as the numerous water columns fitted across the system were designed for lower sided tenders. Crews also reported difficulties with visibility, caused by exhaust steam tending to remain close to the boiler sides, and the steam-operated reversing gear proved to be very inaccurate in use.

With a single locomotive constructed and subject to evaluative testing, many of these problems would have been eliminated prior to volume construction commencing, but that was not to be the way. It was further compounded at the end of the war, with a build of 110 smaller locomotives named in two classes, some of which were not completed until after nationalization. Eventually, all the 'Merchant Navy' class and many of the smaller 'West Country' and 'Battle of Britain' were rebuilt along conventional lines and were to give long, valuable service to their new nationally owned railway, but with many of the revolutionary ideas removed.

As if to compound the idiosyncrasy of his design, the final steam design to come from Bulleid's mind was his even more radical 'Leader' class – a large boiler, centrally mounted firebox and coal bunker mounted on two steam-powered bogies. It had the appearance of the diesel locomotives that were to follow and again plans were sanctioned to build a class of thirty locomotives without evaluating the numerous advanced design features. The project was cancelled before the second locomotive in the class was completed.

Discussions with existing Guy customers, but especially with the West Riding Automobile Company, revealed a number of interesting requirements for the future. Maximum passenger capacity within the limits imposed by the Regulations was a given: low height capabilities without the restrictions of sunken gangways, allowing upper deck seating with a central aisle, was of interest to all operators needing to deal with low bridges. Improved passenger comfort, particularly smooth riding and saloon heating, were seen as desirable, especially as the majority of buses at the time were not fitted with closing doors. Reduced downtime and cheaper maintenance were also naturally important considerations.

West Riding had invested heavily in service facilities that were based on vehicles with the engines positioned traditionally, that is, longitudinally at the front of the vehicle. Remodelling the engineering facilities to handle rear-engined designs would be both expensive and disruptive, so a front-engined design was almost mandatory. A new suspension system to reduce the damage being imposed by the roads would certainly be of interest,

while front entrance and low-bridge construction were both requirements. And it made sense to use commodity sub-assemblies where these were available rather than bespoke designs, so as to reduce both initial and ongoing maintenance costs. Ronald Brookes had discussed his requirements and his solution with the usual suppliers, but all had declined interest. All except Guy. A meeting between Guy Motors and Brookes, apocryphally over dinner and no doubt with outline sketches being made on a napkin, led to an exchange of ideas that were to help influence the direction of Guy's new design.

WULFRUNIAN GOES ON DISPLAY

For 1958, Guy brought an export-only chassis, the Guy Victory Airide, to market, incorporating an underfloor engine, air suspension and disc braking. These developments were to lead the way for the prototype Wulfrunian that was to be shown first at the Scottish Motor Show held in November 1959 in Glasgow. In keeping with the operator

One of the two Wulfrunians to have been preserved is seen at Dewsbury Bus Museum at the end of an extensive restoration. The first impression is of a modern front-entrance bus in the style of Leyland's Atlantean, but closer examination will reveal a series of differences.

The driver's entrance door and extensive grilles suggest that this is something different to the more common Atlantean or Fleetline front-entrance, rear-engined buses.

that had played such a significant role in defining the specification, the prototype chassis had been sent to Charles H. Roe in Leeds to be completed as West Riding fleet number 863. Externally, the appearance was not unlike a Leyland Atlantean, being a large full-fronted box on wheels with the passenger doors ahead of the front wheels. But this was where the similarities ended. Certain features were very obvious: the engine was positioned at the front, alongside the driver and separating him (bus drivers were predominantly male in the 1950s) from the entrance, and

Locating the engine at the front and slightly off-centre created several design issues that needed to be addressed, not least of which was the reduced leg space available for the driver. Access for the driver was through an offside door in the style of a half-cab bus.

BOTTOM: A set of distinctive louvre grilles decorated the front of the Wulfrunian body in conjunction with the combined engine cooling and interior heating system.

therefore a driver's door was positioned in the same manner as would be found on a half-cab; and the staircase was on the nearside, immediately behind the entrance doors. The floor was very low and flat, with the overall height of the finished vehicle at 13ft 4in (4,064mm), even lower than the Bristol/Eastern Coach Works Lodekka with a typical height of 13ft 6in (4,114mm).

Power and Transmission

Production vehicles did not differ from the prototype. The chassis, unlike the simple and robust type used in the Arab, was a complex arrangement of pressings bolted together and utilizing outriggers supporting the body-work. The engine fitted as standard would be the Gardner 6LX, itself recently introduced as an evolution of the long-serving 6LW, which could be fitted as an option, or alternatively the AEC AV590 and both Leyland's O.600 or O.680 could be specified. Located at the front of the vehicle, forward of the wheels, the engine was offset slightly to the offside to increase the boarding space. Drive was taken from the rear of the engine by a short propshaft to the gearbox, the options for which were a semi-automatic based on a standard Self-Changing Gears design, but repackaged by Guy to fit under the floor, or a four-speed manual ZF synchromesh gearbox with

the options of either five-speed or six-speed if required. From the gearbox, a second propshaft took the drive to a drop-centre rear axle. The axle was designed for long life using roller bearings, with the added advantage of reducing noise.

Engine Cooling and Saloon Heating

Engine cooling presented some challenges, with no space to fit a conventional radiator and fan and no practical possibility of venting the hot air, so the system developed at Southampton University by Professor Cave-Browne-

Cave (C-B-C) was instead applied. This system had been prototyped between 1949 and 1951 on a number of Southampton City Transport Guy Arabs running in the city, but was more widely associated with the Lodekka models produced by Bristol Commercial Vehicles. Instead of a large conventional cooling radiator, the C-B-C system instead used smaller radiators placed alongside the destination screen through which the engine coolant was passed. Being positioned in clean air and particularly when cooling the highly thermally efficient Gardner engines, no additional fan was necessary. Cooling air entered via a louvred grille in front of the radiators and could either exit through additional grilles at the side, or be diverted into the saloons to provide fresh air and heating, using a series of baffles to reduce any draughts.

The C-B-C seen in use in Southampton fitted to one of the Corporation's 1952 batch of Arab IIIs, followed by another of the fleet with a conventional cooling system. CW

The C-B-C system was frequently seen on the Bristol/Eastern Coach Works combination as shown here on this 1966 former Hants & Dorset Bristol FLF.

THE CAVE-BROWNE-CAVE FAMILY

Wing-Commander Thomas Reginald Cave-Browne-Cave, CBE, initially served in the Royal Navy as an engineering officer until 1913 when he was seconded to the Royal Naval Air Service, which was to be absorbed into the Royal Air Force. His speciality was the design, construction and operation of aircraft, particularly airships, on which subject he was an acknowledged expert. In 1931, following the end of Government involvement with airships after the R101 disaster, he was appointed as Professor of Engineering at Southampton University, having previously lectured at Imperial College, London. The engineering department at the University grew during his time until his retirement in 1950. He is now remembered for the cooling and ventilation system for buses that bears his name and this came about following a commission from the Ministry of Transport and Society of Motor Manufacturers to develop a system to improve the 'unpleasant and unhygienic conditions' then found on buses.

Born in 1885, the son of Sir Thomas and Lady Blanche Cave-Browne-Cave, Thomas (junior) was elder brother to Henry and the two brothers both shared an interest in aviation, with service in the Royal Navy and subsequently the Royal Air Force. Henry is credited with authorizing the expenditure necessary to allow the development of the Supermarine Spitfire and retired from the Service in the rank of Air Vice-Marshall. Thomas and Henry were brothers to Beatrice (1874–1947) and Frances (1876–1965), who were renowned mathematicians, Frances as a researcher and Beatrice doing work on the mathematics of aeronautics.

The Cave-Browne-Cave family can trace its origins back to 1641 when ancestor Thomas Cave, a royalist, was created a Baronet for services during the English Civil War, and Sir Thomas was the third son of the ninth Baronet. Thomas Reginald Cave-Browne-Cave died at Southampton in November 1969.

Suspension and Braking

Perhaps the most revolutionary aspect of the Wulfrunian was its suspension, front axle, or more precisely lack thereof, and braking. Poor road services and heavy loadings in the West Riding were leading to excessive maintenance costs and downtime resulting from broken leaf springs, and therefore the application of air suspension, which had been used extensively in the United States, was of great interest. The front wheels were independently mounted to the chassis, omitting the traditional beam axle, and suspension was implemented using a rolling lobe air spring mounted inboard of the wheels. The front air suspension was to give the Wulfrunian its characteristic front wheel camber. Steering, typically of its time, was without power assistance. Although Guy

The cutaway chassis detail shows both the disc brake and air suspension system as adopted for the Wulfrunian, although this actual installation is on a Victory chassis, as revealed by the higher chassis line. THE STILLTIME COLLECTION

claimed in its publicity material that the design of the front suspension and steering would 'lighten the task of the driver', the vehicles when they came into service gained a reputation for very heavy steering. The steering box itself was of the recirculating ball type and required six and a half turns from lock to lock to give a turning circle of 62ft (188,976mm).

Rear suspension was, again, by rolling lobe air springs with two at either side, in front and behind the axle, which was itself located using parallel trailing links. Suspension operation on each wheel was controlled by an air valve governed by two master valves situated front and rear. The overall effect was to give a very smooth ride with fast response and very little roll, unlike any other commercial vehicle then on the road in the UK. Test reports documented slight pitching when the brakes were applied, quickly corrected by the suspension system, and a slight tendency to roll when entering a corner, but again this was quickly corrected.

Stopping the bus was to be by disc brakes fitted front and rear, hydraulically operated but with an air-assistance system. Four discs were logically used, one positioned immediately inboard of each wheel and operated initially by two Airpak air/hydraulic servo units, one each for the front and rear braking systems, giving in effect twin circuit brakes split front and rear. A transmission brake was fitted just forward of the rear axle.

Body Features

The Commercial Motor Show models that were bodied by Charles H. Roe set the style for the vast majority of Wulfrunians that were to be built. The very low floor resulted in wheel arches that were intrusive, especially at the front where the location of the engine already limited space for passengers boarding and leaving the vehicle. To improve passenger flow, it was decided to fit the staircase on the nearside, and to maximize space around the boarding doors the stairs were of necessity rather narrow. Limited space for folding doors against the stairwell resulted in asymmetrically split doors being used. The space above the offside wheel arch was used for luggage and once beyond the front wheel arches, the rest of the lower saloon was quite conventional in layout, with double rows of seats apart from over the rear wheels where longitudinal seats were fitted. The floor level either side was raised here to make for easier access for passengers and an emergency exit was located centrally at the back between the rear pair of seats. Upstairs was entirely conventional, with pairs of seats along each side of a gangway and a rear seat for five passengers. Forty-three passengers could be accommodated upstairs, with thirty-two downstairs for a total capacity of seventy-five seated passengers, plus eight standing.

The lower saloon of a Roe-bodied Wulfrunian shows the height of the front wheel arches and the narrowness of the passageway between the engine and nearside staircase.

ABOVE: Positioning the staircase on the nearside reduced the amount of traffic through the entrance, but providing adequate clearance on the front platform resulted in a narrow staircase, which had the benefit of being straight.

LEFT: Looking at the staircase shows the narrow bulkhead at the foot of the stair, against which the smaller portion of the door opened.

To allow the entrance door to lie flat when opened and not obstruct the stairwell, it was necessary for the doors to be split asymmetrically, as can be seen in this image.

Externally, the front of the vehicle exhibited a series of grilles above and below the windscreen. Those above were in connection with the C-B-C cooling and ventilation system, while the offside grille below the windscreen provided airflow to pass over the engine. The nearside lower grille was a dummy provided for symmetry and deleted from later builds. On the prototype, the lower grilles were trimmed in brightwork.

Guy's specifications also mentioned the possibility of fitting a single-deck body and of mounting the entrance door anywhere along the side of the bus. No single-deck Wulfrunians were to appear, but there were to be variations on the theme, which will be covered later in this chapter.

GUY WULFRUNIAN SPECIFICATION

Layout Public Service Vehicle Chassis, suitable for either single- or double-deck coachwork

Chassis type Pressed-steel channel section 8in (200mm) deep pressed from 0.25in thick steel plate, 10× bolted cross-members and outriggers for body attachment

Engine Gardner 6LX details, as specified for the majority of the chassis completed
Type Gardner 6LX
Cylinders 6 in-line
Cooling Water, Cave-Browne-Cave system
Bore and stroke Bore: 4.75in (120.6mm), stroke: 6in (152.4mm)
Capacity 10450cc
Valves 2 valves per cylinder ohv
Compression ratio 14:1
Max. power 125bhp @ 1,700rpm (derated)
Max. torque 405lb ft @ 1,000rpm
Fuel capacity 35gal (159ltr)

Transmission SCG semi-automatic or ZF four-speed manual (optionally five- and six-speed available)
Clutch Fluid flywheel or single dry plate, hydraulic actuation
Gearbox Self-changing gears semi-automatic epicyclic, manufactured by Guy Motors
Overall ratios: Specification for SCG semi-automatic
1st 4.2:1
2nd 2.38:1
3rd 1.59:1
4th 1.00:1
Reverse 6.09:1
Final drive 5.6:1

Suspension and steering
Suspension Guy-Firestone air-pressure system with independent front suspension using twin wishbones and patented control valve system. Single rolling lobe air spring for each front wheel and four in total air springs for rear axle. Telescopic dampers fitted at all wheels
Steering Burman recirculating ball, eight turns lock to lock
Tyres 11.00 – 20in (16 ply) front; 9.00 – 20in (10 ply) rear, provision for 11.00 – 20in to be fitted at the rear

Electrical system 24V, four batteries fitted to rear of chassis
Generator CAV 38amp dynamo, alternator optional

Brakes
Type Clayton-Dewandre-Girling split circuit air over hydraulic with discs for each wheel; air assistance by Airpak servos
Size Front: 15.375in (390mm) diameter discs
Rear: 15.5in (394mm) diameter discs
Handbrake 9in (228mm) diameter drum brake fitted to nose of rear axle

Dimensions
Track
Front 6ft 8in (2,038mm)
Rear 5ft 11.5in (1,816mm)
Wheelbase 15ft 4in (4,673mm) (18ft (5,486mm) for rear and mid-entrance body)
Overall length 29ft 6in (8,992mm)
Overall width 7ft 6.5in (2,292mm)
Front overhang 7ft 1in (2,159mm)
Rear overhang 7ft 1in (2,159mm)
Ground Clearance 5.375in (136.5mm)

GUY WULFRUNIAN SPECIFICATION (*Continued*)

Performance		Bodywork (demonstrator)	
Fuel economy	Between 5.9–15mpg (48–19ltr/100km) depending on load and stopping interval, ranging between two stops per mile and non-stop	Manufacturer	Charles H. Roe
		Seating capacity	
		Lower saloon	31 (optionally 33)
		Upper saloon	41 (optionally 45)
		Overall length	360in (9,144mm)
0–30mph (48km/h)	30sec (*Commercial Motor*, August 1960)	Overall height	161in (4,089mm)

EARLY DELIVERIES

Following the prototype entering service in December 1959, two demonstration vehicles were constructed and registered 8072 DA and 7800 DA. These were bodied by Roe and finished in a gold and black colour scheme, matching the strip of Guy's local football club, Wolverhampton Wanderers. September 1960 saw a good outing for Wulfrunians at the London Commercial Motor Show, with numerous vehicles displayed: two vehicles for West Riding were displayed by Charles H. Roe; Guy Motors showed a bare Wulfrunian chassis; Northern Counties Motor and Engineering Co. showed one vehicle, the first of a batch of three ordered that had been bodied for Lancashire United Transport; and the Park Royal stand displayed an additional Wulfrunian for Bury Corporation, which when handed over was the first Wulfrunian to be ordered by a municipal operator.

Finished in the gold and black colours of its home-town football club, one of the two Wulfrunians built for demonstration use is seen awaiting its next outing at the London Commercial Motor Show. CW

802RTC was originally delivered to Lancashire United Transport in 1961 after being on display at the Commercial Motor Show fitted with a Northern Counties body that followed the general style of the Roe body. It had a short life with its original owner, being withdrawn in 1962, and is seen here with its new owner, West Riding.

With the two demonstrators in much demand around the country, orders for the new vehicle began to flow in. West Riding added to its initial order of fifty with a follow-up batch of a further twenty and a third batch of six to carry single-deck bodies. East Lancashire Coach-builders built a vehicle for West Wales and one for Wolverhampton Corporation, and orders were placed during 1960 by China Motor Bus in Hong Kong, Belfast Corporation and Rotherham Corporation, all of which were subsequently cancelled, as were the remaining two vehicles for Lancashire United.

PROBLEMS ARISE IN SERVICE

Issues began to arise early in service. Despite the reports from road tests suggesting that the steering was not heavy, road crews complained that they did find the steering to be difficult and the cab space for the driver was cramped, a particular problem being that the driver's left leg would be positioned alongside and quite likely resting against the engine cover, immediately behind which was the hot engine and exhaust manifold. Crews also reported feeling travel sick, an unfortunate side effect of the smooth ride. Particular care needed to be taken when driving on road surfaces where adhesion was poor, due to the weight balance being heavily biased to the front.

Problems quickly came to light with the braking system. Inadequate cooling resulted in the pads overheating, requiring them to be changed more frequently and, being unique to this type of vehicle, costs were high. The Airpak system was found to be expensive to maintain, resulting in replacement by more traditional air over hydraulic master cylinders. Restricted flows of cooling air to the brakes resulted in the risk of brake fluid boiling and drastically reducing its efficiency. Extreme caution was required not to apply the transmission brake unless the vehicle had come to a complete stop for fear of causing serious damage.

Use of the C-B-C cooling and ventilation system seemed to be less effective on Wulfrunians than it had been on other types, particularly when compared to Bristol Lodekka types where it was widely used, although again not entirely without issues. Early problems were reported in road tests, where it was noted that the saloon heating element was not efficient until the engine was close to overheating. Maintenance teams found that the engine was difficult to work on, requiring numerous bolts to be removed for access, rather than simply opening the bonnet of a half-cab.

Finally, the load to the front of the vehicle, clearly not helped by the weight of the engine being suspended forward in the frame, created excessive front tyre wear and regular replacement of front suspension components; it will be recalled that one of the original design requirements was to minimize front suspension wear. To help reduce the load to the front of the vehicle, it became usual for the front seats forward of the staircase to be removed, thus reducing the passenger loading.

None of the issues was beyond redemption. Power steering would have resolved the matter of the heavy steering, the use of more conventional air over hydraulic braking solved one of the braking issues, and a different brake pad compound would have addressed the requirement to replace the brake pads on such a regular basis. A full air-brake system would also have overcome the issues that arose with the hydraulic fluid boiling. The difficulty was that time had not been spent on evaluating and working through the problems that could arise when so many new ideas were introduced simultaneously in a new vehicle and in an industry as conservative and risk-averse as passenger transport, bad news tended to spread very quickly, resulting in initial interest in the new vehicle rapidly turning to caution and concern. The next double-decker bus product from Guy Motors reverted to the tried and tested Arab format.

VARIATIONS ON A THEME

Despite the Wulfrunian design being fundamentally for a front-entrance vehicle, one of the features promoted by Guy was that a passenger entrance could be accommodated in any position – front, centre or rear. Accrington Corporation ordered two new vehicles from East Lancs in 1961, both on Wulfrunian chassis, but with rear entrances. These were fitted with Gardner 6LW engines and a ZF synchromesh gearbox, and with no need to accommodate a front entrance, the engine was moved to a more central position and the front wheels moved forwards. A similar mechanical layout was adopted for a single bus, also bodied by East Lancs for Wolverhampton Corporation. Fitted with the more powerful Gardner 6LX engine and semi-automatic gearbox, the entrance to this was positioned just to the rear of the front wheels in the location established for front-entrance half-cab buses. The most radical change to this one vehicle was the removal of the disc brake system and the substitution of more conventional drum brakes, but its operator remained unconvinced and future orders reverted to the more traditional Arab.

One of the two East Lancs-bodied Wulfrunians supplied to Accrington Corporation with rear open platforms. At the time this photograph was taken, the vehicle had been sold to Hertfordshire independent operator Ronsway Coaches and is here on a private hire for an enthusiast group from Eastbourne. ALAN SNATT

Seen on the same trip as the previous image, this view of 35VTF reveals the relatively large driver's cab with entrance forward of the wheel and fuel filler located behind the rear axle. ALAN SNATT

Another 'variation on a theme' example of a Wulfrunian was bodied for Wolverhampton Corporation by East Lancs, now fitted with drum brakes. THE STILLTIME COLLECTION

Seen in later life, after transfer to WMPTE, but retaining the green Wolverhampton livery, 4071 JW is looking very careworn in this picture taken outside the main depot. LES SIMPSON

LATER DELIVERIES

While West Riding remained loyal to the Wulfrunian, other orders virtually dried up, with just three vehicles being delivered to other operators subsequent to 1961. One of these was the vehicle for Wolverhampton Corporation described above, while the other two were bodied by Roe to the style established by West Riding

and delivered to County Motors of Lepton, a concern with whom West Riding had a substantial financial involvement. West Riding remained the only customer for the buses, with twenty-five delivered in 1963 and a final batch of thirty supplied in 1965 with revised front suspension, bringing the total to one hundred and twenty-six, although a final batch of twenty-five for later delivery was cancelled.

West Riding acquired further vehicles, purchasing them secondhand from other operators, who were by this time no doubt more than happy to offload them to a willing purchaser. The West Wales, County Motors and Lancashire United vehicles all came to West Riding, as did the two demonstrators in 1966. The demonstrators had been out of use for some years and were used as a source of spare parts. Eventually, West Riding was to own 132 of the total production of 137 Wulfrunians to have been built. Overall, it was a disappointingly small production run for a vehicle that had on paper shown such promise.

Of the remaining five vehicles, the Accrington rear-entrance buses were both sold to Ronsway Coaches of Hemel Hempstead, Hertfordshire, but were scrapped by 1973. The one example purchased by Bury Corporation was sold after three years and then spent a year with independent operators in South Wales, who subsequently sold it to Wrights in North Wales. Passing then through Ber-resfords of Cheddleton (Greater Manchester), the vehicle

One of the later deliveries to West Riding, BHL360C was new in 1965 and had a short life in service. It is parked here with at least two other Wulfrunians. The small fold-up step just below the registration plate assisted the crew when changing the destination blinds. CW

Viewed in the yard of Crouch End Luxury Coaches, perched precariously on an axle stand, WHL 970 was to be the last Wulfrunian in service. CW

WULFRUNIAN DELIVERIES

YEAR	ORIGINAL OPERATOR	BODYBUILDER	QUANTITY DELIVERED	OBSERVATIONS
1959	West Riding	Charles H. Roe	1	Prototype
1960	Guy Motors	Charles H. Roe	2	Demonstrators
1960	Bury Corporation	Charles H. Roe	1	
1960	Lancashire United	Northern Counties	1	
1960–1	West Riding	Charles H. Roe	12	
1961	West Riding	Charles H. Roe	38	
1961	Accrington Corporation	East Lancs	2	Rear entrance
1961	West Wales	East Lancs	1	
1961	Wolverhampton Corporation	East Lancs	1	
1962	County Motors	Charles H. Roe	2	
1962	Wolverhampton Corporation	East Lancs	1	Entrance behind front wheel
1962–3	West Riding	Charles H. Roe	20	
1963	West Riding	Charles H. Roe	25	
1965	West Riding	Charles H. Roe	30	

was eventually obtained for preservation, but unfortunately was wrecked in an accident when a driver training bus appears to have reversed into it. The two examples that had been purchased by Wolverhampton Corporation had also been scrapped by 1973.

West Riding's extensive fleet survived until March 1972, with a small number sold on for further use. Most were scrapped shortly thereafter. Of those that were sold on, WHL970 was purchased by Crouch End Luxury Coaches, North London, where it was to remain until 1978, the final Wulfrunian in service.

Fortunately, two vehicles have survived into preservation, both from the West Riding fleet. Formerly owned by County Motors, UCX275 and West Riding WHL970 are now in the care of the Dewsbury Bus Museum in West Yorkshire.

THE WULFRUNIAN LEGACY

Guy Motors were facing financial constraints at the time that the Wulfrunian went into production and were perhaps influenced too much by the requirements of one operator. With some simplification, such as coil springs or drum brakes, many of the resulting maintenance costs could have been contained without further development, or a very small fleet built and operated by a friendly

operator might have been used to refine the design and eliminate deficiencies prior to volume production. It could be that the small volumes actually produced may have been considered as limited production at some point, but the warranty costs and poor reputation gained prevented any further investment.

But it would be wrong to dismiss the Wulfrunian as a blind alley in passenger-carrying vehicle design, because many of the features originally seen in it were to become standard fittings in future designs. The smooth ride exhibited set the standards for future bus design, while air suspension and disc braking systems are now almost universal on both buses and coaches.

By 1970, the major British passenger service vehicle chassis manufacturers, Leyland Motors, Guy Motors, Bristol Commercial Vehicles and AEC, were under the common ownership of British Leyland, who were working on a new design for London Transport that would eventually come to light as the B15 Leyland Titan. Although rear-engined, the B15 Titan was another advanced design, again and rather like the Wulfrunian perhaps too advanced for its time, and one that was only adopted in large numbers by London Transport, being seen as mechanically too sophisticated for municipal operation, or for the nationalized National Bus Company. The suspension designs for the Wulfrunian were studied when devising the layout for the Titan and a series of scientifically controlled assessments for ride quality were made using a Wulfrunian, Leyland Atlantean, Daimler Fleetline and the one-off front-entrance Routemaster (FRM), from which selection the Guy vehicle was assessed as providing the best ride. The production Titan looked on paper to be very similar to the Guy vehicle, with a drop-centre rear axle, Gardner power (although in this case the engine was mounted at the rear transversely), independent air suspension all round and air over hydraulic braking. Overall production numbers were higher than the Wulfrunian, but did not exceed 1,200 examples.

A second similar example was to be the Volvo Ailsa of 1975, which followed the Wulfrunian design by employing a front-mounted engine with a set-back front axle and front entrance. Where it differed, though, was by using simple beam axles and leaf springs and by employing a smaller capacity, turbo-charged engine that was physically smaller, thus occupying less space in the entrance of the vehicle. Volume production again was, by the standards of the bus industry, small, with just over 1,000 being completed.

Another example of a front-engined, front-entrance double-deck bus was the Volvo Ailsa, this example fitted with an Alexander body and formerly operated by Maidstone & District.

Chapter 10

THE BEGINNING OF THE END

FINANCIAL DISASTER LOOMS

Throughout the first half of the 1950s, the export market for Guy Motors had been exceptionally buoyant, with the countries of the former Empire and South Africa in particular providing much business for the company. A bout of ill health had resulted in Sydney Guy spending protracted periods in the country to recuperate and it was reported that he had developed a fondness for South Africa, with the passenger records of the Union Castle Shipping Line showing Sydney Guy as a regular First Class passenger between Southampton and the ports of South Africa. Sales of Guy products outside the United Kingdom had been handled in the traditional manner through a network of agents and representatives, who would either purchase and resell, or act as an intermediary between supplier and ultimate user. However, in 1955 the Guy Board agreed to establish direct operations in South Africa, with offices in the major cities of Johannesburg, Cape Town and Durban.

With the large volume of business being achieved in those cities and something in the region of 60 per cent of the company's earnings coming from exports, it was at the time not an unreasonable form of business expansion, providing the opportunity to deal directly with the end customer, with the resulting benefit of more advantageous pricing and more retained revenue to the supplier.

To encourage sales, Guy Motors entered into agreements with finance providers whereby new vehicles would be provided on hire purchase, with the manufacturer acting as guarantor for the debt, resulting in liability for any outstanding debt falling on Guy Motors

in the event of default by the operator. In Guy's case, defaults occurred at a rate higher than envisaged, with the result being an immediate and dramatic impact on the balance sheet.

To compound this unfortunate situation, some transactions were undertaken on a part-exchange basis, with an allowance being made that was in excess of the resale value of the vehicles being offered in part exchange, or, in the case of older vehicles that were really only suitable for scrap, this led to the primary transaction being undertaken at a loss. It was reported that the South African operations, which had previously contributed strongly to the company's overall financial position, deteriorated to the point where they were now costing the company in the region of £300,000 a year.

Taken on its own, the financial situation might have been recoverable, but another drain on the finances was ongoing with the development of the Wulfrunian double-deck bus, as described in the previous chapter. Without the costs of this development, money might have been available to correct the financial situation in South Africa, and without the losses from the southern hemisphere, there might have been sufficient capital available to address the shortcomings that came to light with the new double-decker, which may very well then have turned into what it appeared to be on paper – a design years in advance of the industry and something that addressed many of the difficulties faced by bus operators. But, as history now tells us, it was not to be.

By late 1961, the situation had deteriorated to the extent that the Board was faced with no alternative other than to call in the Receiver and place the company formally into administration. That may well have been the end of a fine product range and an established name, but help was to come from a completely unexpected quarter.

SIR WILLIAM LYONS TO THE RESCUE

William Lyons was another entrepreneurial figure in the motor vehicle industry of the UK, having started his empire in 1922 in Blackpool building sidecars for motorcycles. This business was given the name of the Swallow Sidecar Company, later extending its activities to creating special bodywork on otherwise mundane cars of the 1930s, with small Austins and Standards being a particular favourite for such treatment. From this, Lyons expanded into building his own cars, buying in key mechanical components, primarily from the Standard Motor Company, with whom Lyons was to have a long relationship.

Lyons had a good eye for design and produced many striking designs for his SS cars. Following World War II, the initials 'SS' had taken on totally undesirable connotations, resulting in the business gaining a new name – Jaguar, with early cars continuing to be powered by Standard sub-assemblies before being fitted with Jaguar's own designs from the early 1950s and achieving much success in motor sport, especially at Le Mans.

With a successful product range, a profitable business and cash in the bank, Jaguar was a company looking for expansion and boldly announced an intention to double the size of the business, while wisely avoiding some of the incentives then being offered by the Government to set up new operations in areas of the country that were suffering high unemployment following the decline of traditional industries.

Instead, Lyons and his Board had determined that the key to success was to focus on opportunities that were geographically close to their main base in Coventry. To that end, an agreed offer was made in 1960 to acquire Daimler from its then owner, BSA. While the obvious synergy may have been the upmarket and quality motor cars produced by Daimler, who were a competitor to Rolls-Royce at the top of the luxury car market, Daimler were of course also a long-established constructor of bus and coach chassis, having been established in that business from the earliest beginnings and, with Guy, had kept the country moving during the war years with the construction of utility buses. At the time of the transfer to Jaguar, Daimler were close to completion of their new Fleetline rear-engined, front-entrance bus chassis, a design which, with the rival Leyland Atlantean, would transform the operation of stage carriage vehicles.

Jaguar is usually thought of as a builder of sporting and luxury motor cars such as the E-type seen here, but the company diversified into commercial vehicles with the acquisition of both Daimler and Guy.

Another more typical Jaguar product, a Mark 2 high-performance luxury saloon car.

Daimler's Fleetline chassis proved to be both successful and popular. Walsall Corporation purchased a number of Fleetlines built to their unusual requirements, with a shortened chassis and fitted with bodies by Northern Counties.

With Guy now available for acquisition, having been examined and rejected as a potential purchase by Leyland Motors, in October 1961 Sir William purchased Guy Motors for the princely sum of £800,000. In a series of moves that would today come under very close scrutiny, one week before purchase was completed, a new company, Guy Motors (Europe) Ltd, was formed and all the remaining assets of Guy Motors Ltd were transferred into the new company with the debts remaining with the original business. The staff of the former company were dismissed, but told that they would be re-employed by the new company. A shake-up of the Guy Board resulted in salary cuts and redundancies, with an urgent message given that the existing financial situation was to be rectified without delay. Initially, rationalizations were made to the product range that for the most part only affected the goods vehicles in the range.

A RETURN TO THE ARAB

Guy's next passenger-carrying product was a return to tried and tested simplicity after the advanced technology of the Wulfrunian, with a revised version of the front-engined thoroughly conventional Arab being launched as the Arab V in 1962. Utilizing many of the sub-assemblies from the earlier Arab IV, the most significant change to the Arab V concerned the chassis, which was lowered by 2.5in (64mm) to accommodate the move to forward entrances rather than the traditional rear platform. By reducing the chassis height, it was only necessary to provide two steps in the entrance vestibule. The floor level of the Arab V was claimed to be just 3 or 4in (76 or 102mm) higher than that found on rear-engined, front-entrance designs.

Substantial changes were made to the brakes, which were only offered as a full air-operated system, now using diaphragm brake chambers rather than the cylinder type used on air brake-equipped Arab IV chassis. Gardner as usual provided engines, with the 6LW being the standard model offered, but with both the larger new 6LX or 5LW being available for specific applications. With a standard wheelbase of 18ft 6in (5,639mm), the Arab V chassis was available for bodies 30ft (9,144mm) in length, but both shorter and longer lengths were available for export markets, where single-deck bodies would often be fitted. Transmission was, as usual, either a four-

The low entrance possible with the Arab V chassis is seen here to good effect on this forward-entrance bus operated by Chester Corporation.

speed constant-mesh manual with friction clutch or four-speed air-operated epicyclic with an electro-pneumatic valve block. As was usual practice with Guy, the gearbox was positioned centrally in the chassis and much to the disappointment of traditionalists, the option of a polished radiator was no longer available.

The press release for the new Arab, which was significant as it was the first new model announced from the new

The simple but effective cover for the Arab V sales brochure emphasizes the low chassis height, which provided a low entry point for passengers.

The end of a long tradition – the large exposed radiator frequently capped with the Indian Chief in his war bonnet and the 'Feathers in our Cap' slogan was no longer available with the Arab V, for which model only the new look front as shown here or the similar Johannesburg style was available.

company under Jaguar ownership, emphasized that the Wulfrunian was not being discontinued, but that, simply, the new Arab was being introduced in response to continuing demand for a double-decker chassis of orthodox layout.

An Arab V was on display at the 1962 Commercial Motor Show from a new fleet for delivery in the following year to Wolverhampton Corporation Transport. In total, Wolverhampton took seventy-five Arab Vs in 1963,

two-thirds of which were fitted with traditional half-cab bodies with forward entrances by Weymann and seating seventy-two passengers in total, with thirty-one in the lower saloon. The remaining intake for that year was fitted with Park Royal bodies to similar specification. The change back to half-cabs was in contrast to earlier Arab IV deliveries, which had adopted a flat-front style. These were followed in 1965 with a further thirty-five similarly

GUY ARAB V PASSENGER CHASSIS SPECIFICATION

Layout	Forward-control four-wheel chassis for double-deck bodywork	**Axles**	
Engine	Gardner 6LW as standard, with 5LW and 6LX as options	Front	I section
		Rear	5.6:1
Bore and stroke	Bore: 4.25in (107.95mm), stroke: 6in (152.4mm) (6LX bore expanded to 4.75in (120.6mm)	**Electrical system**	24V, 38A dynamo, battery providing 174AH; alternator listed as an option
Capacity	6LX: 10.45 litres; 6LW: 8.4 litres; 5LW: 7 litres	**Brakes**	
		Type	Foot brake operating drums on all wheels. Compressed air operated using diaphragm type actuators. Front drums 16.5in diameter × 4in wide (419 × 102mm) Rear drums 16.25in diameter × 6.5in wide (412.75 × 165mm)
Transmission	Large single dry plate clutch, or fluid flywheel		
Gearbox	Wilson-type epicyclic, manufactured by Guy Motors		
Overall ratios:		Handbrake	Conventional lever, operating on rear wheels only
1st	4.25:1		
2nd	2.4:1		
3rd	1.57:1	**Dimensions**	
4th	1:1	Wheelbase	18ft 6in (5,639mm)
Reverse	6.2:1	Body length	30ft (9,144mm) (27ft [8,232mm] overall length for double-deckers also available and 26ft [7,925mm]; 32ft [9,754mm]; or 36ft [10,973mm] overall length for single-deck bodywork)
	Four-speed constant-mesh gearbox (not available with 6LX)		
1st	4.51:1		
2nd	2.5:1		
3rd	1.74:1		
4th	1:1	Body width	8ft (2,439mm)
Reverse	4.58:1	Fuel tank	35gal (159ltr)
Suspension and steering			
Suspension	Semi-elliptic front and rear with hydraulic telescopic dampers fitted front and rear		
Steering	Marles steering box		

configured buses, ten of which were fitted with bodies by Strachan and the remainder by Metro-Cammell-Weymann. In 1967, a further thirty-one similar buses followed, again with Strachan bodies that were announced as being supplied to replace the final Corporation trolleybus route from Dudley to Wolverhampton. When all had been delivered, they provided Guy's home town with a fleet of 247 Guy buses.

Strachan, having been active in the bus chassis market from the 1920s to the early 1950s, were making determined efforts to return to that business following a move to new premises at Hamble, in Hampshire. An early product to emerge from their new factory in the second half of 1963 was a seventy-two seat double-deck demonstrator built on a Guy Arab V that featured a sliding forward-powered door. It is considered to be the first, if not

Thirty-five Arab Vs joined the fleet in Wolverhampton in 1965, with the first ten having bodies built by Strachan and the remainder fitted with Metro-Cammell's lightweight Orion bodies as shown here on number 170. All were fitted with forward entrances and seated seventy-two passengers. CW

The Strachan-bodied Arab V was sent on a tour of UK bus operators, including a visit to Sussex, where it is seen here during the early summer of 1964 inside Southdown's bus station in Eastbourne. CW

the only, conventional half-cab design to feature a peaked roof, giving it a very distinctive appearance. This vehicle was to have something of a nomadic life, being demonstrated to various potential operators before finally being sold to Harper Brothers of Heath Hayes.

Other long-term Guy customers purchased the Arab V in significant quantity, despite the general availability of the new front-entrance, rear-engined chassis from other manufacturers. Lancashire United Transport, having taken Arab IVs in 1961 and 1962, were not dissuaded from returning to Guy, even after their experience with their solitary Wulfrunian, taking delivery of sixteen very traditional Arab Vs bodied by Northern Counties with rear entrances and seating seventy-three. They also took a single example of a similar vehicle but with a forward entrance, followed by twelve with forward entrances in 1963, a further ten in both 1964 and 1965, twenty-three in 1966 and a final batch of twenty-five for 1967.

After its service as a demonstrator, the Strachan-bodied Arab V was purchased by Harper Brothers in May 1966 and eventually passed to Midland Red in September 1974. Its life with Midland Red was to be very short, being withdrawn just a month later following a collision between the front dome and a garage door beam. CW

Blue Line continued with the purchase of Guy double-deckers, including this Roe-bodied example that joined the fleet in 1966. It is seen at the end of its route in Armthorpe with its conductress posing alongside. CW

A little further south, Chester City Transport was a committed Guy user, first experiencing the models when operating utility models and having bought only Guy double-deckers between 1953–69, including two second-hand examples from Southampton Corporation. Thirty-two Arab IVs, bodied mostly by Massey, had been delivered up until 1962, with deliveries of twelve Arab Vs commencing in the following year and continuing until 1970. Bodies were by Massey and Northern Counties (Massey Brothers having been merged into Northern Counties in 1967) and all were seventy-three seaters with forward entrances.

The last bus to be delivered in this batch, registered DFM 347H with fleet number 47, chassis number FD77108, was the final Guy passenger chassis to be shipped for the home market, with several of these later

City of Chester's number 46, the penultimate home-market Arab to be delivered, awaits its next duty from Chester city centre, while 37, another Arab V from an earlier delivery in 1965, waits behind.

Another of the final batch of Arab Vs to have been delivered to Chester is seen here on a wet day at the Scottish Vintage Bus Museum at Lathalmond.

vehicles saved for preservation, including number 47. These vehicles remained in service throughout the 1970s, with the final vehicles continuing in service until 1982. However, Chester's patronage remained within what had become the Jaguar group, notwithstanding this now being subsumed into British Leyland, with future double-decker purchases being the Daimler Fleetline model.

An Early Export Model

The West Pakistan Road Transport Board placed an early order for a fleet of thirty-seven Arab Vs for delivery in the first half of 1963. These were shipped in Completely Knocked Down (CKD) kit form for assembly on arrival in Lahore, Pakistan, with each bus chassis packed for the most part in two large wooden crates; large items such as chassis side members were packed separately. All vehicles in this order were powered using 5LW engines.

More export orders for the Arab V followed in 1966, with an order placed by the East Pakistan Road Transport Corporation in Dacca (East Pakistan is now Bangladesh) for forty chassis. Engines in this case were to be AEC AV505 and transmission was by way of a four-speed semi-automatic gearbox built by Daimler, under the model name Daimatic. Once again, these vehicles were supplied as CKD kits.

THE FINAL TROLLEYBUSES

Large-scale closures of trolleybus systems in the United Kingdom started in the late 1950s, while at the same time new vehicles were still being delivered to the remaining systems. With the consolidation of suppliers in the late 1940s into BUT and Sunbeam, owned by Guy Motors, it would fall to Sunbeam to take the honours both as the supplier of the last new trolleybuses to be built for the home market and as the final UK company to be listed as a supplier of trolleybuses. At the London Commercial Motor Show in 1967, the company still listed a range of two- and three-axle vehicles for single- and double-deck bodywork, with bodies of up to 36ft (10,973mm) and seating up to seventy-three passengers.

The final trolleybus chassis to be built for use in the United Kingdom was a Sunbeam from a batch of nine for Bournemouth Corporation, fitted with a Weymann body

seating sixty-five. This batch followed on from deliveries to Reading Corporation, the wonderfully named Teeside Railless Traction Board, Derby Corporation, Huddersfield Corporation and the city of Belfast, although production remained in place for export orders.

What was the cause of the demise of trolleybus systems? Partly it was the lack of flexibility resulting from the fixed infrastructure, which made it difficult to respond dynamically to traffic conditions, for example by journeys being turned around short, or the costs incurred in extending the route network to

The final batch of trolleybuses to be delivered in the UK was supplied to Bournemouth Corporation in 1962, several of which have survived into preservation. 297LJ, one of that batch, is seen here just after the closure of the system.

service the new suburban residential developments that were becoming more common in the late 1950s and early 1960s. Much of the infrastructure was reaching the point at which extensive overhaul and replacement would be required, and there was growing concern at the amount of street clutter caused by the overhead wiring. Another consideration was the nationalization of electricity supply, which had removed the generation of power from the same municipal authorities who would be using the power to energize their transport. Inevitably, systems were closing for these reasons, even though the actual vehicles were still capable of continuing service, resulting in many being sold out of service directly to other undertakings for continued operation. Fortunately for us today, examples of the last vehicles to be built for the home market have survived into preservation, giving people today the opportunity to ride again on these rapidly accelerating and almost silent forms of mass transport.

MERGERS AND ACQUISITIONS

Jaguar Cars continued to expand its operations and in 1963 it acquired ownership of Coventry-based manufacturing business, Coventry Climax. This was a company well known for its diverse expertise in, amongst other areas, small- to medium-capacity high-performance engines that were widely used in motor sport and as the power source for the high output water pumps used by fire brigades as well as constructing forklift trucks. The following year, Jaguar purchased Guy's Wolverhampton neighbour and long-term supplier, Henry Meadows Ltd. Overall, this was to provide Jaguar with a wide range of engineering and manufacturing expertise. The next business transaction undertaken by Jaguar was not to be quite so successful, but first it is instructive to look at other business mergers of the time that were to have an impact on the operations of the Jaguar group of companies.

The Leyland Monster

Leyland Motors, the large Lancashire-based manufacturer of heavy lorry and passenger chassis, had been slowly making acquisitions of smaller companies through the 1950s and had at one time considered, but declined, the opportunity to acquire Guy Motors. In 1946, a joint venture with AEC had formed British United Traction Ltd, Sunbeam's only real competitor in the trolleybus market, and in 1951 Leyland took ownership of Albion Motors, followed by the acquisition of Scammell Lorries Ltd, a company well known for supplying specialist heavy haulage units and military vehicles. Leyland had established a strong reputation with a loyal base of customers, both in the haulage and passenger transport arenas, helped by the skills of their Commercial Director, Donald (later Lord) Stokes.

Flush with cash, Leyland Motors made a venture into the motor car business in 1961 when it purchased the ailing Standard-Triumph business. In 1962, the business was reorganized into a new holding company following a merger with Associated Commercial Vehicles, a group which itself included AEC and Thorneycroft as constructors of commercial vehicle chassis and Park Royal Vehicles and Charles H. Roe, both bodybuilders. In 1965, a minority interest was taken in Bristol Commercial Vehicles and its associated business of Eastern Coach Works, giving Leyland Motors a substantial share of the market for passenger chassis and coachbuilding businesses. Two smaller acquisitions were to follow: Rover, along with subsidiary Alvis in 1966; and the following year specialist vehicle builder Aveling-Barford, whose main interest was in civil engineering construction machinery. This was, of course, occurring at a time when the merger of businesses into larger groupings was seen as good for the country, good for business and good for the economy.

Thus, the market for heavy bus chassis was dominated by the Leyland group and with the Jaguar group playing its part with Guy and Daimler. The lighter end of the market was dominated by General Motor's UK subsidiary Bedford and the Ford Motor Company, which were supplying both goods vehicles and passenger chassis.

British Motor Holdings

While Leyland was occupied with its mergers and acquisitions in the early part of the 1960s, Jaguar was continuing to operate as a profitable and successful business. Car sales were performing well, the E-Type sports car had hugely enhanced its reputation and added a touch of glamour and class to the company, while the heavy Guy lorries were selling in good numbers and both export and home-market sales of Arab V bus chassis continued.

Daimler's Fleetline was selling in large numbers and gaining a reputation as being a superior product to the similar Leyland Atlantean and it was available from its introduction with a drop rear axle, allowing a low-bridge body with conventional seating to be fitted upstairs, something that was not possible with early Atlanteans.

Jaguar reported a net profit of £1.6 million, so the business was of interest to other motor manufacturers, one of which had been Leyland. Sir William had declined offers, but was to entertain merger talks with the British Motor Corporation (BMC), another group that had been put together in 1952 from William Morris' Nuffield group and the Austin Motor Company. At the time, BMC were in the ascendancy, with technically advanced cars such as the Mini and its larger brother, the 1100, for many years the bestselling car in the UK, along with simpler, more traditionally engineered, but ageing models such as the well-loved Morris Minor. BMC had an extensive but overlapping dealer network and ample manufacturing facilities, but also suffered from fragile industrial relations and a multitude of unseen problems arising from the merger that had created the company and which had not been resolved. BMC had recently acquired Pressed Steel, which produced the bodyshells for Jaguar, and an ongoing concern for Jaguar was the threat that supplies of bodyshells could be at risk. Such thought was not without precedent, as BMC had earlier purchased another pressing works, Fisher & Ludlow, which quickly ceased the provision of supplies to BMC's rivals.

Guy's Arab V remained a popular choice in export markets, especially South Africa, as demonstrated by this locally bodied Arab operated by Springs Municipal Transport.

It was in this environment that Jaguar and BMC were to merge to create BMH – British Motor Holdings – in 1966. Cash was generated from this merger to provide further development and launch funding for the forthcoming XJ6 luxury car, but at the cost of giving up independence and shackling the company to a business that was almost to cause the downfall of the entire Jaguar group.

BMH becomes BLMC

Stimulated by the rush for mergers, with Government support and encouragement, 1968 saw BMH merge with Leyland Motors to form the British Leyland Motor Corporation. It rapidly became very clear that the volume car business within BMC, the Austin and Morris brands, were painfully short of new model development. In addition, production was badly costed, meaning that many vehicles were being sold at a loss, while industrial relations were a cause of almost daily headlines in the press, with BLMC rapidly becoming a national laughing stock and the reputation of its quality products damaged by association. Rationalization of products, brands and facilities resulted in assets of the acquired companies being closed and brands that were not original to Leyland being discontinued. A victim of this policy was to be Guy.

THE SLOW DEMISE OF GUY

With all the merger and acquisitions background, sales of Guy bus chassis in the home market became very slow, with just one product, the Arab V, available. In an effort to modernize the bus fleet and encourage the move to driver-only operation, the Government in the UK introduced a Bus Grant scheme that provided initially 25 per cent, later increased to 50 per cent, of the capital cost of new vehicles, provided that they were compliant with a specification defined by the Government. While many operators, who were in general a conservative group, would prefer the tried and tested front-engined traditional chassis such as the Guy Arab V, Leyland PD3 or AEC Regent V, the financial advantages of the Bus Grant were such that moving allegiances to models such as Atlanteans, Fleetlines and, when it was available on the open market, the Bristol VR, where overwhelming. With complete irony for Guy Motors, the Wulfrunian would have met all the requirements to qualify for the Bus Grant and satisfy the needs of a longitudinally mounted forward-located engine.

In the export market, it was a different matter, with the company maintaining its reputation for rugged, hard-wearing products that were straightforward to service and able to cope with the arduous conditions that could be encountered. Experiences with early rear-engined

The two buses here, both new at the same time as the final Arabs and delivered to Chester Corporation, demonstrate the changes that had taken place in bus design as the 1960s came to an end, making the traditional front-engined, half-cab design look decidedly out of date. On the left is a Daimler Fleetline, originally ordered by Birmingham Corporation but delivered to the West Midlands Passenger Transport Executive, and to its right is a Bristol VR new to Midland General.

buses had not been so promising, as the low ground clearance, a clear advantage when operating on paved city streets by providing an easy single-step entrance, created problems on gravel roads, and transmission failures were very common. With little competition, the Victory and Warrior continued to sell, especially in Africa and would shortly be re-branded.

GUY CONQUEST

With Guy Motors now part of the Jaguar Group, it came as little surprise that future product plans would be closely coordinated to prevent direct competition between companies in the same group. Following on from the success of the rear-engined Fleetline, a new single-deck chassis was developed to the new maximum dimensions of 36ft (10,973mm) length and 8ft 2.5in (2,500m) width, initially designed with an in-line, turbo-charged rear-mounted engine of Daimler's own design. First shown at the 1962 Commercial Motor Show, the design proved to be of interest, but potential customers expressed a desire for a change of power to use the Gardner 6HLX, even though this would require substantial redesign of the chassis to accommodate it. But at the time, Gardner were selling every engine that they could build and no further capacity was available, resulting in Daimler widening their search for a suitable motive unit. A solution was found with the US engine builder, Cummins, with part of the deal calling for Jaguar to build the engines, for which the facilities of Henry Meadows Ltd, which were being acquired at the same time, would be ideal. That part of the plan was not to come to fruition, with Cummins ultimately building the engines at their own facilities in Scotland and the north-east of England.

The Cummins engine, of V6 format and 9.63 litres capacity, was both smaller in capacity than the 10.45 litres of the Gardner 6LX and significantly higher in power output, producing 192bhp as against the 150bhp available from the most powerful version of the Gardner. Minor revisions would be required to the chassis, but the resulting design was suited to both the stage carriage single-deck bus design for which it was originally intended, and also, with different gearing made possible by the engine's higher output, as a long-distance coach on the growing motorway and high-speed highway networks.

Sold as the Daimler Roadliner and as the Guy Conquest in certain export markets, particularly the Benelux countries where Guy held a strong reputation, initial interest was strong. Unfortunately, deliveries of bus bodied Roadliners rapidly gained a reputation for poor reliability, with the transmission being operated at the limit of its performance and the weight of the rear engine causing stress cracking in the chassis. This was not helped by the almost universal fitting of dual-entrance coachwork, with commensurate loss of rigidity. Engine problems also came to light, even when derated to 150bhp, in the stop-start nature of local bus work, with problems including overheating sometimes resulting in pistons disintegrating, cylinder liners cracking and fuel injectors blocking. Ultimately, it was concluded that the engine, despite its high power and compact size, was not suitable for the rigours of bus operations. The obvious substitutes from Gardner or Leyland would not physically fit, so alternatives were then either a Perkins V8 or an AEC V8 810, with a capacity of 13.1 litres and a power rating of 270bhp; an engine which was also to prove to be under-developed and equally challenging in bus installation.

Fortunately, although described as a chassis for both bus and coach use, the Guy Conquests that were produced for export markets operated in environments that were less stressful on the transmission system and less likely to cause the overheating difficulties. Its first public appearance was at the Brussels Motor Show in January 1965, having been seen the previous year in London with its Daimler badges and the following year at the Dutch show in Amsterdam.

An early order came in September 1966, handed over at the British Commercial Motor Show, and this was for four Conquest chassis, with Cummins engines fitted and the option of rubber suspension. Three types of suspension were offered on this chassis, the alternatives to the rubber system being a full air system, or traditional steel springs. The customer, who had never previously purchased any British bus chassis, was the nationalized Chemins de Fer Vicinaux (SNCV), the largest bus operator in Belgium. The vehicles were intended for high-capacity bus operation and were to be fitted with high-density bodywork built by Jonckheere and accommodating up to eighty passengers, many of whom would be standing.

Despite slow sales, the business that had now become British Leyland persevered, with sales efforts for the

Guy's sales brochure for the Conquest included two artists' sketches of completed vehicles: a touring coach in mountain scenery and a bus in a modern urban environment. GUY MOTORS

GUY CONQUEST PASSENGER CHASSIS – KEY DETAILS

Layout	Rear-engined, front-entrance 36ft (10,973mm) (chassis suitable for bus or coach bodies)	**Axles**	
		Front	Single-piece steel-forged, located with Panhard rod
Engine	Cummins V6, later Perkins V8 and AEC/BL V8	Rear	Located with Panhard rod; numerous axle ratio options, single and two-speed
Power output	Cummins V6: 192bhp Perkins V8: 170bhp AEC/BL V8: 270bhp		Single speed: 5.29:1, or 6.5:1 Two speed: 5.14/7.02:1, or 4.87/6.65:1, or 4.11/5.6:1
Capacity	Cummins V6: 9.63 litres Perkins V8: 8.4 litres AEC/BL V8:13.1 litres	**Electrical system**	24V, high-output alternator fitted as standard, battery providing 140AH
Transmission	18in fluid flywheel		
Gearbox	Air-operated, semi-automatic epicyclic	**Brakes**	
		Type	Air-braked, foot brake operating drums on all wheels
Overall ratios:			Front drums 15.5in diameter × 6in wide (394 × 152mm)
1st	4.5:1		
2nd	2.53:1		Rear drums 15.5in diameter × 8in wide (394 × 203mm)
3rd	1.64:1		
4th	1:1	Handbrake	Conventional lever, operating on rear wheels only
Reverse	5.53:1		
Suspension and steering		**Dimensions**	
Suspension	Full air with automatic self-levelling front and rear; Metalastik rubber-bushed suspension, or traditional steel springs as options	Wheelbase Body length Body width Fuel tank	18ft 6in (5,639mm) 36ft (10,973mm) 8ft 2.5in (2,500mm) Bus: 35gal (159ltr) Coach: 45gal (204ltr)
Steering	Worm and nut		

Also in the brochure were two technical illustrations: that on the left showing the detail of the air suspension system; and on the right, the compact installation of the Cummins V8 engine. GUY MOTORS

conquest and regular attendance at the Benelux shows, but curiously the new AEC Sabre coach chassis were also shown alongside the Conquest, two chassis that were in many respects very similar, built by what was in reality the same company competing for the same market. Clearly, it was not just with private cars where BL considered internal competition to be a cogent business strategy.

GUY ENDS WITH VICTORY

Alongside the passenger vehicle business, Guy had continued to construct heavy lorries, with the last new models, introduced under Jaguar ownership, given the model name Big J, with the J standing for Jaguar. The Big J chassis was incorporated into the Victory during the latter part of the 1960s, at which point it was to be the only front-engined heavy-duty bus chassis for export markets in the range. With the Warrior being withdrawn and with the final Arab chassis being built towards the end of the decade, the Victory, now marketed as the Victory J, became the *only* Guy-designed passenger vehicle to remain in the range, as the Conquest was a Daimler product in all but name.

Despite the Victory J being designed and intended only for single-deck bodies, the difficulties being encountered with the new range of rear-engined buses called for desperate measures, resulting in the South African City Tramways Group, the major transport undertaking in the

country, arranging for the local body builder, Bus Bodies S.A. Ltd, to modify a Victory J chassis to take a double-deck body. The project was very successful and led to orders for new Guy chassis to be fitted locally with the new double-deck bodywork. An initial order for eighty chassis was placed in 1973 and within two years over 100 double-deck Victories were in service on the roads of South Africa.

A further 152 of the revised Victory Mark 2 design followed quickly, with the front axle moved forwards and the entrance door now located behind the front axle to reduce the load on the front wheels and lessen the previously high tyre wear and heavy steering. In 1978, the Guy name was lost, with the chassis now branded under the parent company of Leyland. Although many Victory chassis buses now operated on city roads, the suspension retained its rugged go-anywhere design, although an improvement to the braking system incorporated a hold facility to allow the vehicle to be stopped for passenger boarding without exhausting the air supply. Accompanying these revisions came a new double-deck Victory chassis, now known as the Victory 2, series II, which incorporated a mix of assemblies from the Leyland Worldmaster chassis and from the Guy heritage.

A significant factor in encouraging Leyland to create the final Victory chassis came from Dennis, a rival from the early days of Guy Motors who were winning orders for high-capacity, front-engined double-deck buses from the Kowloon Motor Bus Company in Hong Kong – a

A pen sketch of a high-capacity service bus illustrated a press advertisement for the Guy J-type bus chassis. Careful examination reveals that no opportunity has been lost to promote other products within the Jaguar company – both cars in the background are Jaguars. GUY MOTORS

The two Busaf-bodied single-deck buses show the high ground clearance, although the entrance steps may have been vulnerable. The buses are operating in the Johannesburg and Pretoria areas, with Rustenburg being a town to the west.

territory that had long been a substantial source of business for Guy. Orders for 152 of the new Victories, with power coming from a 180bhp Gardner 6LXB engine transmitted through a Voith D851 fully automatic transmission, were placed with Leyland, with subsequent orders in following years. Announcing the order in *Commercial Motor*, it was noted that the order was 'hardly a vote of confidence' for Leyland's rear-engined bus designs which 'have not proved able to stand up to conditions in Kowloon'.

The other major bus provider in Hong Kong, China Motor Bus Company, historically a loyal Guy customer who had taken substantial numbers of Arabs, continued their loyalty with a fleet of Victory double-deckers assembled locally, as was the usual practice, with high-capacity bodies provided by Walter Alexander.

Guy Motors exhibited for the final time at the 1980 Commercial Motor Show, now held in its new home at Birmingham's National Exhibition Centre, and the Fallings Park Works was closed in 1982. Production of the Victory moved to Leyland's main production plant at Farington in Lancashire, with production finally ending in 1986 after a production run of around 800 Victory chassis had been completed at the Lancashire Works.

With that, the final links with the business originally established by Sydney Guy in 1914 were ended after seventy-two years. Of the Works at Fallings Park, very little remains, the site having been redeveloped into modern industrial units. The only tangible link is an area named Guy Motors Industrial Park.

LEYLAND WORLDMASTER – THE OTHER GO-ANYWHERE BUS CHASSIS

With sales totalling over 20,000 units, the Worldmaster was one of Leyland's most successful products and sold worldwide, with substantial markets in Africa, South America, Australia and the Indian subcontinent, all places where it would come head to head with Guy. Sold in three wheelbases to give overall lengths of 30ft (9,144mm), 33ft (10,058mm) and 35ft (10,668mm), the chassis was powered using a Leyland O.680 horizontal engine, with drive through a semi-automatic gearbox. The chassis was of substantial ladder construction and was designed to have two options for ground clearance, with a lower clearance usually specified for use on paved roads. Newer Leyland models, such as the Leopard, reduced the Worldmaster to sales in environments requiring extreme heavy duty chassis, where it found tough competition with Guy's Victory.

A double-deck Victory 2 is seen here operating around Cape Town in an all-over advertising livery.

Now residing at the Scottish Vintage Bus Museum at Lathalmond, LV36, now with a UK registration, is an example of the large fleet of Victory 2 buses that operated in Hong Kong.

Chapter 11

GUYS IN PRESERVATION

Whenever a red-painted half-cab, open rear platform double-deck bus is seen at an event for classic vehicles, it is certain that 'there's a Routemaster' will be heard from someone, even if the bus is a Bristol or a Guy, such is the dominance and popularity of former London Transport vehicles in preservation. Fewer Guys have survived from the end of their working lives into preservation, but sufficient do survive to provide an interest, including the last Guy Arab to have been produced for the UK domestic market, delivered to Chester Corporation and now a resident in the North West Transport Museum in St Helens on Merseyside. Without exception, the owners and custodians of those vehicles that have survived into preservation are enthusiastic about their buses and have willingly helped in the creation of this book.

In no particular order, the following details just a selection of the vehicles that have been preserved, including the joys and challenges of their ownership and operation. Despite their age, some remain licensed for commercial operation, carrying fare-paying passengers on special occasions or for private hire.

LONDON TRANSPORT GUY GS

Of the eighty-four GS country buses built for the country area service of London Transport, it is frequently commented by enthusiasts that about eighty-five have survived into preservation, such is the enthusiasm for these small vehicles. The truth, though, is that around thirty of the fleet escaped the cutter's torch and found new lives either in preservation, or, in a small number of cases, conversion into caravans or mobile homes.

Exactly halfway into the fleet, GS42 was new in November 1953 and delivered for service in Surrey, based at the garage in Dorking. A transfer in February 1955 took it to Garston, near Watford, before going in 1962 first to Amersham and then to Hemel Hempstead. Following a period in storage, a short time at Windsor then found it back in Dorking between 1966–8, before heading back to Garston, where it found use as a driver trainer. In March 1972, it was to work on the final country area routes to be operated by a Guy Special and was finally withdrawn immediately afterwards. In the summer of that year, GS42 was purchased by a school in Ashford, Middlesex, in the south-west of London, having provided nineteen years of service for London Transport. At the end of the following year, it was acquired by its current owner, Geoff Heels, who resides close to the bus's original home in Surrey, and it has been a regular visitor to many events, running days and rallies all over the country since then. Geoff has taken the bus on long journeys, including trips to Scotland, where it has proven to be a reliable form of transport; it is maintained in as-new condition.

The simple and robust style of construction ensures that age-related failures are minimal, but despite the large inventory of spares originally stocked at London Transport depots and sold on once the vehicles were withdrawn from service, parts that do fail are becoming more difficult to locate. Even though the Perkins P6 engine was widely used, its adaptation for use in the GS included a number of unique parts that are difficult to obtain – and the P6 engine has, in any case, been out of production for about sixty years.

Numerically close to GS42, GS40 and GS41 were sold in January 1961 to West Bromwich Corporation where

On show at the Basingstoke Festival of Transport in 2017, GS42 has been owned by Geoff Heels for longer than it was owned by London Transport, and is regularly seen at rallies where it always attracts many admiring visitors.

The view seen through the front of a GS is one that many rural passengers will have seen in the 1950s. The interior colours of green and cream with red beading were common on London buses of the era.

The open driver's cab on GS42 shows the simple, workmanlike layout. Like most other buses built for London, the driver was provided with a well-padded seat.

GS41 survived until the middle of 1972, after which it went for scrap, but GS40 was more fortunate and has survived. Having been converted first to provide transport for handicapped people in the West Midlands borough, it found itself back in bus service in 1963, then being used as a vehicle for the Sports Department of the authority, prior to final withdrawal towards the end of 1973. Passing through a succession of owners in preservation and now repainted in West Bromwich colours, it can frequently be seen at the open air Black Country Living Museum situated in Dudley.

Another example that was preserved in the livery of its subsequent operator prior to a repaint back into the more familiar green is GS2, registered as MXX302. Sold in 1963 to Southern Motorways, it was used for much of its life with this company on a short service between

Originally GS40, and one of the two vehicles sold to West Bromwich, this example was spared scrapping and now provides an internal transport link at the Black Country Living Museum in conjunction with a tram and trolleybus circuit.

GS2 ended its working life with Southern Motorways in Emsworth, Hampshire, in whose livery it is shown here. CW

Emsworth and the residential area of a Royal Air Force station at Thorney Island, before final withdrawal and being saved for preservation in 1972.

Finally, the first and last members of the fleet, GS1 and GS84, have also been saved for preservation.

TROLLEYBUSES

Is a trolleybus an easier subject for preservation than an internal combustion-powered vehicle? This is a question that was posed to members of the East Anglia Transport

Museum at Carlton Colville on the outskirts of Lowestoft in Suffolk, where a working trolleybus circuit has been established and is one of the few places where preserved and restored trolleybuses can be seen running under the wires. Lowestoft is a town that amongst its other claims to fame is the most easterly point of the British Isles and was formerly home to the extensive Eastern Coach Works business; this second claim gives the town a strong connection with UK passenger transport, with ECW-bodied vehicles having formed the backbone of the nationalized fleet.

The response was that from the viewpoint of the chassis and bodywork, there is very little difference between the two types of vehicle, but when the form of propulsion is considered, on balance it was thought that a diesel-powered vehicle presented fewer difficulties in restoration. The specialist knowledge and skills to undertake

refurbishments to high-output electrical motors and the associated control gear is less widespread than the knowledge to rebuild and maintain diesel engines; the electrical motive units were built in far smaller numbers, and replacement parts to rebuild motors that have degraded over the years are more difficult to find, frequently requiring bespoke engineering and specialist reconstruction. On the other hand, the number of moving parts in an electric motor is far lower than in a large diesel engine.

Preserved Sunbeam Trolleybuses

Sunbeam came under the control of Guy Motors in 1948, after which date all Guy and Sunbeam trolleybuses were sold under the Sunbeam name. With Sunbeam being the supplier of the final such vehicles to be provided for the UK home market, it is perhaps appropriate that several have been preserved, including the very last to be delivered to Bournemouth Corporation, and can be seen running at Carlton Colville, at the Black Country Living Museum in Dudley and at the Trolleybus Museum located at Sandtoft close to Doncaster in Yorkshire. It is testament to the original build quality of the chassis, control equipment and coachbuilding of these vehicles that despite intensive use during their service lives, it has

ABOVE: One of the last trolleybuses to be built for the domestic market, a Sunbeam F4A with a Burlingham body, originally delivered to Reading in 1961 and transferred to Teesside in 1969 after the Reading system closed, is seen shortly after repainting into its final colour scheme at the East Anglia Transport Museum.

RIGHT: Another example from the end of domestic trolleybus production and also at the East Anglia Transport Museum is a Bournemouth Corporation MF2B with a Weymann body incorporating the unusual Bournemouth style of front doors and an open rear platform.

2206 OI was the final trolleybus to be purchased by Belfast Corporation and is a Harkness body on a Sunbeam F4A chassis. Again, this is seen at the East Anglia Transport Museum.

been possible to restore and maintain them in a condition that represents how they appeared at the prime of their service, and to the efforts of the volunteers who ensure the vehicles remain available to ride on.

'Happy Harold' – A Go-Anywhere Trolleybus

From the operational viewpoint, a diesel bus can go anywhere the driver chooses, subject to supplying it with an adequate amount of fuel, but a trolleybus requires the overhead wiring infrastructure, which restricts its operation to a limited number of sites. One of a very small number of Guy trolleybuses to survive in preservation is from the former Hastings fleet. As part of a modernization of the earlier tramways, Hastings Council obtained a fleet of fifty single-deck and eight double-deck Guy BTX six-wheel trolleybuses. The double-deck buses were unusual in that they were open top and, apart from a number of conversions further along the coast in Bournemouth, were unique in the world. All except one of the double-deckers were scrapped by 1940, when more modern vehicles were

Retaining its power-collecting poles, Hastings & District converted this vehicle to diesel operation after it was withdrawn from use as an overhead maintenance vehicle, which permits it to travel under its own power. It is seen here in the 1980s. CW

introduced to replace them, while the single-deckers were loaned to other cities in the UK as the population of coastal towns like Hastings was partially evacuated for fear of invasion. The surviving vehicle, registered DY4965, was converted into a mobile platform to allow it to be used to service the overhead wiring.

It was returned to use as a trolleybus for the celebration of the Coronation of Her Majesty Queen Elizabeth II in 1953, part of a long tradition of trams and trolleybuses being decorated with additional overall lights to celebrate significant national and local events. Following the Coronation, a large placard of a warrior from the era of the Norman Invasion was placed above the driver's cab and, avoiding any allusion to William the Conqueror, the bus became unofficially known as 'Happy Harold' in

The rear view shows the open platform and exposed staircase of 'Happy Harold'. cw

commemoration of the vanquished King Harold. Capturing the imagination both of residents and visitors to the seaside resort, 'Happy Harold' became a popular attraction in the town and remained in service until the closure of the system in 1959. But the closure of the system was not to be the end for DY4965, as Maidstone and District Motor Services, then owner of the former Hastings Tramways, installed a Commer TS3 two-stroke diesel engine and transmission so that 'Harold' could continue to provide open-top seafront services until 1968, when a fire was to see the vehicle withdrawn and placed into storage.

Further restoration saw the bus take part in the 1977 Queen's Silver Jubilee celebrations before the 1987 hurricane struck, destroying the shed in which the trolleybus was stored, along with the upper deck of the vehicle. More restoration was to follow, with extensive work to the rear axles and braking system, with the result that the vehicle first built in 1928 was still to be seen ninety years after it was first delivered.

EARLY ARABS

The Provincial Arabs

Two early Arabs, one originally delivered to Red & White, found their way to Provincial, more properly known as the Gosport and Fareham Omnibus Company. EHO 228 was delivered directly to Provincial with a Weymann utility body in October 1942 and was one of the vehicles to be rebodied locally in Portsmouth by Readings. It was the first Guy bus to be operated by Provincial and one must presume that experiences were positive, as a number of later Guy vehicles were obtained in the future. This vehicle, now rebodied, remained until 1970, when it was sold, but it was purchased back in 1983 for preservation. It was kept for a period at the Working Omnibus Museum Project in Portsmouth and is now owned by First Bus, while being made available for the Provincial Society.

Red & White were also supplied in October 1942 with an Arab I, complete with a low-bridge Duple utility body and registered EWO 467, as the final vehicle in a small batch of four. In 1951, Red & White dispatched the bus to the local Brislington Body Works (BBW), part of the

Provincial 55, an early utility Arab, was rebodied locally by Readings, in which form it has been preserved. It is seen here on display next to a later rebuild at a rally in its home town of Gosport. BOB JACKSON

extensive Bristol Commercial Vehicles enterprise, itself part of the nationalized British Transport Commission, and to whom Red & White had recently sold their interests where the bus was fitted with a new low-bridge body. Having been sold to a private operator in the South Wales valleys, it then found its way to Hampshire in 1965, the first of six Guy Arabs to be operated by Provincial that had begun their lives with Red & White. Also withdrawn for scrap in 1970 and sold to a local breaker, it was rescued for restoration and preservation, before eventually finding a home in a museum in Cardiff, South Wales, where it was found that the bodywork had deteriorated beyond repair. Stripped of its bodywork, the bus is now kept as a rolling chassis in the museum as an exhibit to demonstrate the construction methods of a typical mid-twentieth century double-deck bus.

Three more Guy Arabs that once gave service with Provincial have also survived into preservation. EHO 869, Provincial's fleet number 57, is now owned by The Provincial Society and has been extensively restored by members of the society. Also rebodied by Readings of Portsmouth, this vehicle is mentioned earlier in Chapter 7. Fleet number 17, one of the rebodied flat-fronted buses, has also survived to preservation, owned by a group of Provincial enthusiasts. A later Arab III built in 1949 for Red & White, fitted with a low-bridge Duple body, arrived in Fareham in 1967. Originally obtained

for a contract concerned with transporting construction workers to major developments on the New Forest side of Southampton Water, the vehicle did make occasional journeys on normal stage carriage services, but was not a popular vehicle with passengers or crews who were not used to sunken-galley, four-abreast seating, low-bridge buses. Eventually it was painted in an all-over yellow colour scheme and became a driver trainer bus, before withdrawal and selling for scrap. Rescued and repainted in its original Red & White livery, the vehicle is now an exhibit at the Transport Museum, Wythall.

Finally, one of the Provincial Deutz-engined buses has escaped destruction and was last reported to be in the United States, where, amongst other uses, it has seen service as a mobile wine bar.

Some Other Early Arabs

As a result of the necessarily poor-quality original construction materials and subsequent rebuilds, few of the utility Arabs have survived into preservation with their original bodies. One that, on first view, appears to have survived is a former Plymouth Arab II that forms part of the collection at the Scottish Vintage Bus Museum at Lathalmond, but appearances can be deceptive, as the current vehicle is not all that it appears to be. The chassis

RIGHT: Provincial's convertible 'coach bus' is also seen at a rally in Gosport, parked alongside a Royal Blue express coach from the early 1960s.

BELOW: With a chassis from a Plymouth bus and a body from one that was delivered to Northampton, CDR679 represents the utility bus style that provided transport during the conflict years of World War II. It can be seen at Lathalmond.

is one of slightly more than 100 Guy utility buses delivered to Plymouth Corporation between July 1942 and the end of hostilities; it was registered as CDR 679, with a low-bridge body by Charles H. Roe. It ran around the city and naval port until 1957, when it was sold to a large Cornish independent bus operator, Grenville Motors of Camborne. Once its life there came to an end, the bus found its way to a farm in Essex, where it was put into service as a flat-bed lorry to haul straw and hay, the original body having first been removed.

Rescued and transported to its current home in Scotland, a replacement Duple utility body was fitted in 2001, the donor being a Daimler CWD6 that was supplied to Northampton Corporation in the early part of 1946. There is a strong connection between the original Plymouth utility bus and Scotland, in that a number of former Plymouth vehicles were later transferred to AA Motor Services, a group of independent bus companies operating services in the south-west of Scotland. Accordingly, after a period wearing the original drab grey utility bus colour, CDR 679 was repainted in the green livery of that operator, prior to a more recent repaint into the livery of W. Alexander & Sons of Falkirk.

A Weymann-bodied Arab II was delivered to Swindon Corporation in July 1943, part of a small fleet of utility buses that were operated in the area. This example was given fleet number 51 and registered DHR192. When withdrawn from service, the bus was selected

A front three-quarter view of CDR679 shows the quality of the restoration of this vehicle.

for preservation by the British Transport Commission and was kept at the original Transport Museum located in Clapham, south-west London. It is unrestored and retains its original wooden seating. With the closure of the Clapham Museum and the relocation of the exhibits, DHR was to find its way to the National Museum of Science and Industry, but rather than being on display, it forms part of the collection that remains in storage at a former RAF airfield at Wroughton, close to its original home of Swindon. The collection has been opened for visits on rare occasions, but is usually inaccessible for visitors. An image of this vehicle appears in Chapter 4.

Two other unmodified early Arabs that reside in museums are more accessible. One can be seen at the Transport Museum at Wythall as a static exhibit in the process of restoration to its original condition. Delivered late in 1944 as part of a batch of forty, all powered by Gardner 5LW engines, this example, like most of its contemporaries in the Midland Red fleet, is fitted with a Weymann body. Early in its life, as soon as hostilities ended, changes were made that included replacing the original wooden seats with more comfortable upholstered seats. In March 1955, the bus was fitted with a new body by Brush. The new body included modifications to the front of the vehicle, resulting in the cab front being extended to finish flush with the radiator, and the nearside mudguard was revised so that this too matched the flat profile of the cab

front. New windows were fitted, now with sliding ventilators, and in this condition the bus remained in service with Midland Red until it was withdrawn from service at the end of October 1955, moving a little to the south for continued service with Warners of Tewkesbury, who fitted doors to the rear entrance.

Ten years later, the bus was finally withdrawn from service and, like many redundant buses at that time, it was to find a new use with a local motor club, before being moved to the Cotswold Gliding Club. Gliding clubs in the 1970s found redundant buses to be useful vehicles for conversion into winches for launching the aircraft, for mobile airfield control towers and sometimes as social clubs. In 1975, it was saved for restoration and rebuilding to its original condition. It was acquired by the Transport Museum in Wythall in 2010.

The second is the only surviving former London Transport utility Guy to have been preserved in the United Kingdom as originally built as a bus. From the large fleet of 435 such buses that once operated in the metropolitan area, just five were to be preserved. Of these, one of the batch that was rebuilt and rebodied for Edinburgh Corporation still exists and will be discussed below; G348 was rebuilt as a lorry after being withdrawn from service in 1953 and is believed to be under restoration; while two former London buses in this series, G346 and G434, were shipped to the United States,

having been in service until 1967 in that stronghold of Guy vehicles, Burton-upon-Trent, and at one time were known to be kept as part of a museum collection in Houston, Texas. With so many of the fleet being exported, it is possible that some still remain and it must be hoped that one day, no matter how unlikely, a long-neglected barn will reveal a complete and restorable former London Transport Guy utility.

G351, with the registration HGC130 and fitted with a Park Royal body, was built in 1945 and delivered to London Transport to enter service early in 1946. It was to spend all of its career in London based at the garage at Upton Park in the east of the Greater London area until it was sold, along with five others, including the two that were to be exported to the United States, to Burton, where it would become number 70 in that town's fleet and remain in service until 1967. At this point it was obtained for preservation and shown at many rallies in its original London Transport colours before being donated to the London Bus Museum, where it has been extensively rebuilt to the same condition as when it was first delivered. A regular visitor now at many events, the bus can usually be seen at the London Bus Museum located within the historic Brooklands race circuit complex in Surrey.

ABOVE: **Inside the museum at Wythall, HHA26 is being restored to as-built condition.**

Now resident in the London Bus Museum, G351 is the only survivor from the once extensive fleet of London Transport Guy utility buses known to have survived in original form. LONDON BUS PRESERVATION TRUST

A Preserved Edinburgh Rebuild

With the acquisition of the former London Transport utility buses for rebuilding, Edinburgh Corporation entered into an agreement that at the end of their second lives, they would be scrapped. Only one deviation from this requirement was made and that was for a vehicle that was put aside for conversion as a tree lopper, as a result of the responsibility for tree cutting being transferred from the City Engineer's Department to the Transport Department. In

Viewed from the rear, the rebuilt buses had a completely traditional appearance and were functional rather than stylish. The distinctly curved rear window is unusual.

ABOVE: JWS594 started life as a London utility bus prior to refurbishment and rebuilding with the body shown here. The false flat front is apparent when viewed from this angle.

Looking inside the lower deck, the transverse front seat is obvious, as is the missing rear offside longitudinal seat that has been replaced with a luggage rack. Being fitted with a straight staircase, there was insufficient room to fit the usual seat over the wheel arch.

the end, the conversion was never undertaken and the bus was sold for preservation, now being part of the collection at the Scottish Vintage Bus Museum at Lathalmond.

Delivered as one of a batch of sixty-five fitted with Park Royal-built bodies, registered GLL 577 and given the fleet number G77, the bus entered service in the summer of 1943. Withdrawal from London service came in early 1952 and it was one of the vehicles selected for sale to Edinburgh following overhaul and rebodying, entering service in Edinburgh in 1953 and operating until the late 1960s.

ARAB IIIS IN PRESERVATION

Arab IIIs have survived into preservation in respectable numbers, reflecting the large amount constructed and their withdrawal from service at a time when interest in saving the nation's transport heritage was gaining momentum. Many of the double-deck buses to have survived are fitted with bodies either constructed by Park Royal, or by Guy Motors to the Park Royal design.

Southampton Arab IIIs

With Southampton Corporation operating a large post-war fleet of Arab IIIs, it is no surprise therefore that several remain and two are regularly seen both at classic vehicle shows and running in free service. LOW 217, an Arab III powered by a Gardner 6LW engine with a manual gearbox, first entered into service with the Corporation Transport Department in September 1954 as part of the final batch of 150 similar vehicles. It wore the fleet number of 71, that fleet number having previously been carried on a 1937 Leyland TD5 which had been withdrawn just a few months earlier. Although it was not numerically the final vehicle of the type in the fleet, that honour falling to number 73, it was to be the last Guy vehicle to remain in service in Southampton, the remainder of the Arab IIIs going prior to 1973 and the UF single-deck buses all being withdrawn in 1973. Its final use was to be on a short service between Shirley on the north-western edge of the city and a large new housing development at Lordshill. Once eventually withdrawn from working on stage carriage work in the summer of 1975, the bus remained licensed for private hire work.

With the deregulation of the bus undertaking in 1986, number 71 was transferred to the ownership of Southampton City Council along with a similar vehicle, FTR 511, which had been converted to open top for tours around the docks in 1966.

Number 71 was one of the fleet of Southampton buses that was experimentally modified with the C-B-C system in 1957, which remained fitted until late in 1969, when a conventional engine radiator system was reinstated. A close examination of the forward upper panels shows where the grilles to exhaust excess warmed air were once fitted. Although still owned by Southampton City Council, both LOW 217 and FTR 511 are cared for by the Southampton and District Transport Heritage Trust. Two further examples of the once extensive maritime city fleet are also preserved by private owners: one in original closed top condition; and the other that was converted to open top at the same time as FTR 511.

One of the final Park Royal-bodied Arab IIIs to operate in Southampton as part of that extensive fleet has been preserved. This was one of the vehicles that was modified as part of the C-B-C system development and close examination shows where the vents were later panelled over.

LOW 217 seen again, next to an open-top Southdown vehicle of an earlier generation.

While it was usually seaside towns that converted vehicles for open-top services, Southampton provided trips to the Docks using converted Guy Arab IIIs, an example of which is seen here. This bus also transported the victorious Saints football team on the occasion of their FA Cup win in 1976.

Back to Lathalmond

Two Arab III examples that operated in Scotland are usually on display. As the reader will recall, the Arab III was introduced first as a single-deck, half-cab chassis, an example of which was delivered new to Edinburgh Corporation Transport in September 1948 as part of a fleet of ten similar vehicles with a single-deck, thirty-five seat rear-entrance bus body built by Metro-Cammell, registered as ESG 652 and given the fleet number of 739. The bus has a number of unusual features, including a full-width rear-ward facing seat along the front bulkhead and a smaller transverse rear seat, partially protected by a wrap-around to the rear bodywork extending partly forwards across the

entrance. For a vehicle built just for stage carriage operation, the quality of the finish is remarkable, with various art deco fittings and the interior roof finished in a decorative material known as 'Alhambrinal'. Now fully restored and operational, the vehicle spent some of its final years with Edinburgh Corporation Transport as a driver trainer.

The second Arab III is a double-decker dating from a little earlier in 1948, fitted with a fifty-six seat high-bridge body. It has an appearance that at first glance is similar in outline to the usual Guy Motors or Park Royal body, but was actually built by Cravens, one of a batch of twenty-five similar vehicles that were delivered to W. Alexander & Sons Ltd that year. Although Cravens were better known for their main business of constructing wagons and coaches for the railways, significant numbers of both motor bus and trolleybus bodies were constructed, including a number of RT bodies for London Transport and bodies for the bus and tram fleet in the company's home city of Sheffield.

Red & White Arab III

The Red & White group, with its main operating base in South Wales and the surrounding border areas of

ABOVE: Edinburgh Corporation ran a fleet of Metro-Cammell bodied single-deck Arab III buses, an example of which is preserved at Lathalmond.

The interior of the Edinburgh single-deck buses: quite grand for a service bus. Note that cigarette stubbers are fitted to the backs of the rear seats, smokers being requested to occupy the rear seats.

England, but with subsidiary operating companies in the south of England, was, in 1950, when it finally sold out to the recently nationalized British Transport Commission, one of the largest independent bus companies in the United Kingdom, with a total fleet strength of around 750 vehicles. The company's first introduction to Guy vehicles, like many others, was with the arrival of the utility Arabs. Deliveries commenced in the summer of 1942 and continued until the end of 1945, by which time the fleet consisted of thirty-eight Arab Is and Arab IIs, some of which were transferred between the individual operating companies and nearly all were rebodied between 1949–52, after which most gave service into the early 1960s.

Immediately post-war, a fleet of thirty-three Gardner 6LW-powered Arab III chassis fitted with low-bridge bodies built by Duple was purchased, along with additional similar but high-bridge bodied vehicles. All but two of the low-bridge buses were used in the main Red & White fleet, with the remaining vehicles being distributed throughout the group operating companies. The Duple bodies were finished to a high standard, with rear platform doors and luggage racks above the lower nearside seats, and the vehicles were regularly used on long-distance services, including that running between Gloucester and Cardiff. Two are known to have survived into preservation, one of which can be seen at the Transport Museum at Wythall. New in 1949, it was registered HWO 334 and given the fleet number L.1149 in Red & White's unique numbering style, in which L signified a low-bridge bus and 1149 showed it to be the eleventh such vehicle to have been taken into the fleet in 1949.

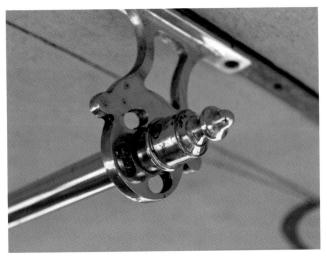

A close-up image showing some of the detail of the fittings inside the Edinburgh single-deckers.

A rear view showing the wrap-around corner offering some weather protection for rear-seat passengers.

Seen at Lathalmond, an Arab III with a
body by Cravens.

A rear view of an Arab III with a
Cravens body, parked close to an
earlier utility-bodied Guy displaying
the much simplified method of
construction of the latter.

The bus found its way to Provincial in Fareham in 1967,
where it was used on contract work prior to conversion to use as a driver trainer vehicle, before eventual
withdrawal in 1971. It now forms part of the static collection in the museum, but is usually easily accessible
for viewing.

Lancashire United Express Coach

In 1951, Lancashire United Transport purchased a
fleet of ten Guy Arab III single-deck chassis fitted with
forward-entrance coach bodies by Charles H. Roe
seating thirty-five passengers. Although various dual-

The varnished wood and moquette-upholstered seats fitted in the lower saloon of the Cravens-bodied Arab give the bus a level of comfort that was not common at the time.

HWO334 is seen here when first restored and returned to Red & White livery. CW

purpose vehicles had been purchased by the company, these were their first dedicated coach vehicles and were used for express coach services, especially on the arduous routes across the Pennines to the north-east of England, excursions and private hire. One of the fleet was given the number 440 and registered as MTJ 84

and was to remain in service until 1965, when, following withdrawal, it was purchased for use by a petroleum company. It was eventually acquired for preservation in 1972, finding its way to a specialist operator of classic coaches and appearing from time to time in period TV dramas.

This Arab III coach, new to Lancashire United Transport, survived into active preservation and remains licensed for the carriage of passengers for hire or reward.

A change of livery for the Lancashire United Transport Arab III coach seen in the previous figure saw the roof painted white, which no doubt had a beneficial effect on the temperature inside the vehicle in the summer.

Delivered at a time when underfloor-engined coaches were becoming available, the half-cab single-deck coach was looking decidedly old fashioned within a few years of being delivered, but that very factor today has a distinct charm and attraction in its current use for events such as weddings. Running a classic public service vehicle, or as they are more correctly called today, a passenger-carrying vehicle, is no less onerous than running a modern fleet, with the requirement for properly licensed and trained drivers who are both willing and capable of controlling a vehicle with a gearbox lacking synchromesh and no power steering. The operator must obtain the appropriate operator's licence and continue to satisfy the authorities that the business is run in compliance with the strict undertakings attached to the licence, and there is no relaxation in the rules requiring the vehicle to undergo a thorough Ministry examination annually and regular safety checks. To add further to the operator's worries, the vehicles are in the main part unique and a specific vehicle will have been chosen for the event, so the unexpected non-appearance of the chosen vehicle due to mechanical failure is likely to result in a disappointed customer; something that is less of a problem with a modern fleet where a substitute can more easily be found.

Arab IVs and Vs in Preservation

With production of the Arab IV not ending until 1963 and domestic market deliveries of the Arab V continuing until 1970, it is not surprising that the final versions of the Arab have survived in larger numbers. Of the 301

A Birmingham Standard Arab IV in the attractive livery of its owner, seen at the Transport Museum at Wythall.

The side view of a Birmingham Standard Arab IV shows the small window positioned alongside the staircase.

Arab IV buses that were operated by Birmingham City Transport, two have been preserved at the Transport Museum at Wythall, representing the early and later deliveries to the fleet. JOJ 533 was delivered in 1950 and ran in service for twenty-seven years until finally being withdrawn in 1977, its service life having been extended due to a shortage of newer vehicles and spares to maintain them throughout the 1970s. When finally

withdrawn from Acocks Green garage in October 1977 from what had become the West Midlands Passenger Transport Executive, it was the oldest of the traditional fleet of vehicles to remain in service, in recognition of which it was immediately purchased for preservation by a group of employees.

JOJ 976 is a little newer, joining the fleet in 1953, by which time the body design had undergone minor re-

The lower deck of a Birmingham Standard. The straight staircase has reduced the seating by one passenger downstairs, with the offside longitudinal seat reduced to two passengers.

Upstairs on a Birmingham Standard, a single seat is fitted at the top of the staircase, providing more space for circulation.

visions, being extended to 27ft (8,232mm) in length; the windows were all a little deeper, and economies were made in the upholstery, where leathercloth replaced moquette for the upper seating. This bus also passed to the ownership of the new West Midlands Passenger Transport Executive on its formation in 1969, but in view of its anticipated withdrawal, it was to retain its Birmingham livery until it was finally retired from service at the beginning of 1972. Purchase for preservation followed in the summer of the same year and in January 1983 it was transferred into the care of the Transport Museum in Wythall, which continued the work of its former owner in returning the vehicle to a high standard, culminating in it obtaining the necessary certification to be used as part of the hire fleet. Both vehicles are fitted with the standard Birmingham body built by the Metropolitan Cammell Carriage and Wagon Company (MCCW) and feature the enclosed radiator styling to the front of the engine.

Lancashire United Transport continued to be a loyal customer of Guy Motors and continued to add new Arab IVs and Vs during the 1950s and 1960s, despite a less than encouraging experience with the solitary Wulfrunian

that formed part of the fleet. The first batch of ten Arab IV chassis fitted with Weymann bodies was delivered in 1951, and with the exception of 1955, batches varying between seven and thirty-three chassis were purchased each year until 1967, with just short of 250 Arab IV and Arab V vehicles delivered during the period, in addition to quantities of underfloor-engined vehicles. Of these, all but a handful were supplied with bodies by Northern Counties in Wigan, conveniently close to the main operating centres for Lancashire United. With the transition to the Arab V chassis, the move was made to forward entrance. An example from the Lancashire United fleet can be seen at the North West Museum of Road Transport located at St Helens in the north-west of England, and at least one vehicle has been retained in service by a heritage operator.

Meanwhile, on the south coast, two Arab IVs that were formerly part of the City of Exeter fleet and one from the fleet of Southdown have been preserved. Of the Exeter fleet, one of these, registered TFJ 808, has been retained for heritage commercial operation, based in Worcestershire. New in November 1956, the bus is fitted with a

The last of the Northern Counties Arab V buses delivered to Lancashire United with a rear-platform entrance, fleet number 135, has been retained for active preservation and is seen here in service providing transport around Silverstone Motor Racing Circuit, carrying a full load of seventy-three and leaning gently as it rounds a curve.

fifty-six seat body by Massey. UFJ 296 is a year newer and is fitted with a Park Royal body, also seating fifty-six passengers. In 1970, the Exeter undertaking was transferred to Devon General and shortly afterwards this vehicle was transferred to Western National, where it became a training vehicle prior to withdrawal for preservation in 1980. Both vehicles can be seen at rallies in their original Exeter green liveries.

In the first half of 1956, a fleet of Guy Arab IV buses, fitted with fifty-nine seat Park Royal bodies, joined the Southdown fleet. The bodies were superficially of similar appearance to those fitted to the extensive fleet of

Running on a heritage bus service, a former Exeter Guy Arab is seen here. TFJ808 is fitted with a Massey body. cw

Also running on a heritage bus service, another former Exeter Guy Arab, UFJ296, has a Park Royal body. cw

LEFT: Former Southdown Arab IV number 547 has been restored to a very high standard and is seen here under the canopy of Eastbourne railway station during a running day event. CW

BELOW: From the earlier batch of Arab Vs operated in Chester, number 35 is now kept in the North West Transport Museum in St Helens. One interesting feature seen here is the extended handle to work the destination gear. This removed the requirement for the conductor to perch on the front of the bus while reaching for the handle, which was usually positioned directly under the canopy.

London RT buses, other than being of five-bay construction and possessing platform doors. From this batch, one has survived into preservation, registered PUF647, formerly car number 547, as all Southdown vehicles were officially designated 'cars' by the company. Unusually, this one vehicle was fitted with a two-part sliding platform door, rather than the more usual folding type. Sold for further service in 1970, the bus has been in preservation since 1973 and can be seen regularly at events in the south of England, especially in its former operational area.

The Chester Arabs

With the final Guy Arab chassis supplied for the home market to the City of Chester, it is fortunate that both the first and the last buses in the final batch to be delivered have been preserved, along with one similar Guy Arab V from a batch supplied in 1965. All are fitted with forward-entrance bodies with sliding doors and seating seventy-three passengers; the earlier bus has a body constructed by Massey Brothers that is visually similar to bodies built by Northern

Counties, the company that was to take over Massey in 1967. The two later buses both carry bodies by Northern Counties. The earlier bus, fleet number 35, registered FFM135C, and the final bus, number 47, registered DFW347H, can both be seen at the North West Museum of Road Transport, while number 42, the first of the final batch and registered XFM42G, is kept at Lathalmond. Number 42 was the final half-cab bus to be withdrawn from service in Chester during 1982, a year after its sister, number 47.

For a city with a relatively modest fleet size, Chester buses are well represented in preservation, as Guy Arab IV, registered RFM641 and given the fleet number 1, the first Guy Arab IV to enter service in the city, has also been preserved. Part of a batch of three vehicles delivered in 1953, all fitted with rear open-platform entrance bodies built by Massey, Chester's coachbuilder of choice, number 1 stayed in normal service until 1976, after which it was downgraded, like so many survivors, to a driver training vehicle. It was relicensed as a PSV in 1981 and used for promotional activities, until it was eventually designated for preservation.

LEFT: The rear view of 35 shows the lower saloon emergency exit as an opening door on the offside of the vehicle. Compare this with the rear of the later vehicle from the final batch.

Number 42 was the final half-cab bus to be withdrawn from service in Chester and is seen here at Lathalmond.

ABOVE LEFT: In the later buses, the emergency exit was positioned centrally at the rear, as seen here on Chester 42.

ABOVE RIGHT: RFM641 was the first Arab IV to enter service in Chester and after a long life has also been preserved. It has a body by Massey and was thoroughly conventional, with a rear-platform entrance.

UNDERFLOOR SURVIVORS

The final four production Arab LUF chassis were all purchased by Harper Brothers of Heath Hayes, located on the edge of Cannock Chase in Staffordshire. The company was an operator of both local bus services and coach hire. Two were fitted with the very attractive Burlingham Seagull bodies, while the other two were dispatched to Willowbrook where Viking coach bodies were fitted. All four vehicles have survived into preservation, with the two Willowbrook examples repatriated from the Republic of Ireland and donated by the former owner for restoration at the Aston Manor Road Transport Museum at Aldridge. The two Burlingham-bodied examples were sold into preservation in 1975, shortly after Harper's business was sold to Midland Red, and can be seen frequently at events, especially in the West Midlands.

Also to be found at the Transport Museum in Aldridge is a former Arab LUF demonstrator fitted with a Saunders-Roe lightweight single-deck, front-entrance bus body. Although this was to be the only Guy to be fitted with this type of body, Saunders-Roe had an established business in constructing coachwork for buses, especially batches totalling 250 standard London Transport bodies for fitting to the RT fleet, although they were better known for the company's interests in aviation as the leading constructor of flying boats and hovercraft. Registered LJW 336, the chassis was built as a prototype LUF to evaluate the possibility of reducing the weight of the earlier UF chassis. After fulfilling its use as an evaluation and demonstration vehicle, the bus was sold to Blue Line, an independent bus operator located in Doncaster, South Yorkshire. After a long service life, the interior was removed and the remains of the bus converted to an office prior to preservation. While many LUF chassis were powered with 5-cylinder engines, this example is equipped with a Gardner 6HLW, but the electrical system is a 12V installation that still causes limitations in its operation.

Guy Motors built a demonstrator Warrior lightweight, underfloor-engined coach that was given the code of WUF and fitted with a Burlingham Seagull body. The power source for this example was originally a Meadows 4DHC.330 4-cylinder engine developing 85bhp

This former Guy demonstrator fitted with a Saunders-Roe (SaRo) bus body is now a resident at the Aston Manor Road Transport Museum. Although the SaRo bodies were relatively common on Leyland chassis, this example was to be unique on a Guy chassis. It is seen in the livery of its eventual owner. MARTIN FISHER

With its interior now replaced, the interior of LJW336 provides a simple but adequate form of transport. The rearmost seats are reduced in width to fit into the rear corner of the body and not obstruct the emergency exit. The luggage shelves are unusual for a service bus, but would permit use for private hire.

This large 'ARAB' badge, complete with the Guy Motors emblem, decorates the front of the bus.

Registered SJW515, this bus was purchased by Dodds of Troon in south-west Scotland towards the end of 1957 and operated in everyday service for twenty years. Problems with the Meadows engine came to light within the first three years and enquiries were made to Guy Motors regarding replacing the original engine with an AEC AV.470 unit and compatible gearbox, which the letter reproduced (*see* p.200) suggests as being technically feasible but expensive. In due course, the engine transplant did occur and the power to the vehicle is now provided by an AEC unit, which itself was undergoing an overhaul at the time that the photographs illustrating this coach were taken during the late summer of 2017.

Following withdrawal, the coach was subjected to a comprehensive restoration and refurbishment to return it to its original condition, after which it was to spend several periods of time on hire and finished in the livery of other operators around the country. It is a rare example of a preserved vehicle, which, other than its initial period as a demonstrator, has remained in the ownership of its original owner.

Running such a vehicle is no different to any other 1950s era coach, with the major difficulty being finding crews who are willing and able to drive a vehicle so different to the modern bus or coach, lacking as it does power steering and requiring considerable skill to master

from its 330cu in (5.4ltr) capacity. Gearing was through a five-speed Meadows constant-mesh gearbox with over-driven top gear, and early reports praised the good fuel economy that this combination achieved. Braking was by a full air system with split operation that was reported as being one of the 'first British designs to incorporate a twin-circuit, air pressure braking system', according to a report published in *Commercial Motor* in February 1957.

Seen inside the depot of Dodds of Troon, SJW515 has had a long life with this company, where it remains licensed for public hire.

An offside view of the Seagull-bodied Warrior owned by Dodds of Troon. Unlike the similarly bodied Arab LUF, there is no air grille and a simplified Guy mascot and badge has been fitted.

The rear view of the Burlingham Seagull body had been revised to create an appearance that bore some resemblance to the style used by Duple on some Vega and Britannia coach bodies. Burlingham would in due course be acquired by Duple.

its non-synchromesh, unconventionally laid-out gearbox, especially when simultaneously handling modern traffic conditions. Major refurbishments have not presented in-surmountable problems; as an example, re-upholstering seats is in principle the same as would be needed for a modern vehicle, but the period moquette seat covering material is only available to special order, requiring a special process run at the weaving mill and a minimum order that is sufficient to refurbish several vehicles.

Another Warrior lightweight underfloor model, this time a bus version, has survived and for a period of time was in the ownership of a heritage operator. The body-

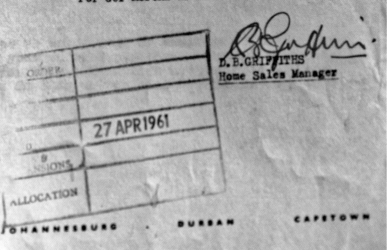

GUY MOTORS LTD.

Telephone: WOLVERHAMPTON 31241-8
Grams and Cables: 'GUYMO' WOLVERHAMPTON

6SH/DBG/MG

WOLVERHAMPTON
E N G L A N D

24th April,,1961.

Dodds (Coaches) Limited,
72 Portland Street,
TROON,
Ayrshire,
Scotland.

Dear Sirs,

re: Guy Coach

Thank you for your letter dated the 14th April and we have noted your remarks regarding recurring trouble with the Meadows DC/330 engined Guy Coach in operation in your fleet.

We have investigated with our Service Department, the possibility of a conversion as mentioned in your letter and would advise you that although this is possible, very considerable modifications are necessary. The estimated cost of such a conversion, including the supply of the A.E.C. AV.470 engine and gearbox is well over £1,000.

If you require any further information and a more detailed analysis of the parts required, our Service Department will be pleased to go into the matter further.

Yours faithfully,
for GUY MOTORS LIMITED

D.B.GRIFFITHS
Home Sales Manager

27 APR 1961

ALLOCATION

LONDON · JOHANNESBURG · DURBAN · CAPETOWN

A copy of the correspondence between Guy Motors and Dodds, reproduced by kind permission of the company, reveals that difficulties with the Meadows engine came to light early in the life of the coach.

The driver's area of the Seagull-bodied Warrior is quite conventional in layout, other than the layout of the gears.

Fully refurbished, the interior looks as good as new. The middle rows of seats have been removed to allow access to the engine.

SJW515 has worn many liveries since new. In this image, it is finished in the colours of Seagull Coaches, who were the first customer for this body style and from which the model name is said to have derived. cw

work for this vehicle was provided by Mulliners of Birmingham, who had a healthy business supplying bodywork for car manufacturers in the Coventry area and especially to Standard-Triumph, who would eventually take over the business. Their large vehicle experience dated back to the utility bus period of World War II, when they were providing bodies for the only permitted single-deck buses at the time built on to Bedford's OWB chassis. With the coming of peace, the company was under sub-contract to Duple, constructing later single-deck buses on the OB chassis. This was to be followed by many military contracts to provide coachwork for buses operated by the Army, Navy and Royal Air Force, again almost exclusively on Bedford chassis, but now the larger SB type.

Registered 647BKL, this bus was supplied new to Leybourne Grange Hospital in Kent, an establishment for people with learning difficulties, then it was passed to Phillips Coaches of Shiptonthorpe, close to Market Weighton in the East Riding of Yorkshire. Phillips Coaches operated an eclectic fleet, painted in an all-over grey livery used mostly on contract work, and once the buses had reached the end of their serviceable life they were frequently left parked on the operator's premises, from whence this vehicle was purchased for restoration. It was to have a short moment of fame when, repainted into the red livery of United Automobile Services and given a fictitious fleet number, it appeared in the Yorkshire Television series *Heartbeat*.

Seen here in the colours of its final operational owner, Phillips Coaches, Guy Warrior 647 BKL has appeared in the TV series *Heartbeat* painted in United's red livery. The simple body style is typical of Mulliners, who built a large number of vehicles for the UK military services.

WULFRUNIAN

For a vehicle that was built only in modest numbers, most of which could be found with a single operator and one which gained such a poor reputation for reliability in normal service, it is fortunate that any Guy Wulfrunians have survived at all. Just two have survived and both are now kept under the auspices of the West Riding Omnibus Museum Trust, one at their premises in Dewsbury and the other at a remote site, but which can often be seen running at events held in Dewsbury. In 1963, WHL970 was new to the fleet of West Riding Automobile Company, another claimant to the title of the largest independent bus operator, and initially it was allocated to a fleet replacing a former tramway route, for which purpose it was painted in the red and white livery that it now wears in preservation. The final Wulfrunian to remain in service, after being sold by West Riding in 1969, it passed between several independent operators in Scotland prior to finding its way to Crouch End Luxury Coaches in north London, who kept it until 1978 when it was first acquired for preservation.

The work on the vehicle has been extensive, requiring new panelling and a complete bare metal repaint to the original livery, which is now magnificent. Gearbox and engine overhauls have been relatively straightforward, as these are commonly used items, but work to the braking and suspension systems has required the specialist remanufacturing of items including brake callipers. In addition, the opportunity was taken during the restoration to replace the wiring and overhaul the cooling system.

The second Wulfrunian was new in September 1960 and was originally one of two supplied to County Motors of Lepton, a company that had a complicated ownership following a sale by the founders in 1927; this resulted in ownership being split among the West Riding Automobile Company, Barnsley & District Traction (which later became Yorkshire Traction) and Yorkshire Woollen District Traction. The influence of the West Riding company led to County Motors

One of the two surviving Wulfrunians, seen outside the Museum in Dewsbury. ANDREW BEEVER

The other surviving Wulfrunian is seen in an almost identical location to the previous figure at Dewsbury.

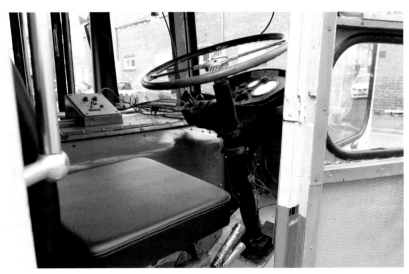

LEFT: A rear view of the Roe body fitted to all but a few Wulfrunians.

ABOVE: A frequent criticism of the Wulfrunian was the small space provided for the driver. The cab area of WHL970 is seen here with the electrical system being renewed.

placing an order for two Wulfrunians to the same specification as those supplied to West Riding. The two new vehicles were given fleet numbers 99 and 100 and both passed to West Riding in 1963, where they were to join the bulk of the production Wulfrunians. Number 99, registered UCX275, was renumbered and given fleet number 995, then renumbered again in 1970, becoming number 487 in the West Riding fleet. In common with the majority of the West Riding fleet, it wore the normal green and cream livery.

UCX275 continued to operate in service until the final day of service for the remaining, depleted Wulfrunian fleet and on Monday, 20 March 1972, the date on which the fleet was withdrawn from service, it was to be the last vehicle to be driven back to the depot at Belle Isle in Wakefield. It can therefore claim to have been the final Wulfrunian to have been in service with West Riding.

A HONG KONG VICTORY IN SCOTLAND

Production of Guy bus chassis for the domestic market may have ended with the final deliveries to Chester, but Arab V

chassis continued to be built for the export market, especially for Hong Kong, where they were perfectly suited to the arduous hilly terrain. The final Guy bus chassis, although now officially described as a Leyland Victory 2 in deference to the marketing strategies of the new corporate business, continued to sell in large numbers to both China Motor Bus and Kowloon Motor Bus in Hong Kong, fitted with high-capacity bodies locally assembled. One of the last to be built entered service in November 1980, having been assembled by China Motor Bus from a kit built by Walter Alexander. It was finally retired from service in November 1998, having covered an estimated 900,000 miles (1.44 million km) in everyday service in Hong Kong. Powered by a Gardner 6LX engine and automatic transmission, fleet number LV36 had a capacity for one hundred and two seated passengers, sitting five abreast on hard-backed seats, and standing capacity for an additional six passengers.

Following its withdrawal, the bus was donated to the Scottish Vintage Bus Museum at Lathalmond and a long journey by vehicle transporter ship commenced to bring the bus first to Southampton, following which a shorter road journey of 460 miles (740km) took the bus to its new home in Scotland. It is frequently in service

Another vehicle at the museum in Lathalmond, this Victory 2 with Alexander body gets regular use as a shuttle providing transport around the extensive site on open days.

Bearing some similarity with the Wulfrunian, the Victory 2's driver was provided with an access door to avoid having to climb over the engine to enter the cab.

The upper deck of the Hong Kong bus showing the five-abreast seating on hard-backed seats. Large sliding windows provide ventilation.

From the rear exit doors, looking forwards, the narrow space between the front wheel arch and the engine and gearbox can be seen.

providing a shuttle around the museum site, but has been given a UK registration so is legal to be used on public roads, although its height can be a problem with trees. A commemorative plaque is fitted inside the bus recording the event and acknowledging the support of Walter Alexander and Volvo Bus, who had by then acquired all the Leyland bus-building interests.

FRANKY TOURS VICTORY COACH

Guy built the Victory chassis for the export market, with many being built in trambus format for use in Commonwealth countries. The underfloor-mounted engine chassis version of the Victory, designated MUF for Mediumweight Under Floor, sold in moderate numbers to European operators, who were drawn to Guy Motors because of the flexibility shown in accommodating operators' specific wishes in terms of engine and transmission. One example, supplied to Franky Tours of Bruges in Belgium during 1961, has survived and at the time of publication is undergoing restoration work at the Aldridge Transport Museum. Fitted with an air-assisted ZF six-speed synchromesh gearbox and powered by a Leyland O.680 horizontal engine, the owners chose a local, market-leading coachbuilder, Jonckheere, to fit a coach body suitable for long-distance touring work.

Following an accident in 1965, a new body was fitted by the equally famous Van Hool company and the coach remained in service operating across Europe until it was downgraded to provide transport for schools towards the end of its life, before eventual retirement in 1979. But rather than being scrapped, the interior of the coach was stripped out and it was put to further use as an office. When the business was finally closed, owner Raoul van der Geutche offered the vehicle to the museum. Belying its age, the coach is in remarkably good condition mechanically, requiring just the normal recommissioning works that follow a protracted laying-up period. The bodywork is also in good condition, although some items of trim and detail fittings are missing and will need to be found or remanufactured, as will much of the interior. But, when completed, it will be a magnificent and unique example of the final Guy underfloor coach design.

Following an accident, Franky Tour's Guy Victory shown in the centre here was fitted with a new body by Van Hool.
FRANKY TOURS/MARTIN FISHER

Franky Tour's Van Hool-bodied Guy Victory, now repatriated from Belgium and undergoing restoration. MARTIN FISHER

INDEX

AEC
  Bridgemaster 137
  Q-type 135
Albion Motors 164
Arab III enhancements, air brakes,
    preselective gear change 82
Arab III for London Transport 83, 84
Arab IV General Specification 97
Associated Commercial Vehicles Ltd,
    creation 74
Aston Manor Road Transport Museum
    196–197, 205

Barton, Thomas 46
Bellis and Morcom 9, 10
Birmingham Corporation
  first purchase 26
  single deck rebuilds 47, 48
  standard design 95
Birmingham Technical School 9
Black Country Living Museum 175
BMMO (Midland Red) 137
Bournemouth Corporation 60th
    anniversary 164
Bristol 'Lowdekka' 137
British Leyland Motor Corporation 166
British Motor Holdings formation 165
Brookes, Ronald 137
Brooks, Leila 12
BSA 156
Bulleid, Oliver V. S. 139
Burton-upon-Trent, early Arab shipments
    51, 52
Bus Grant 166

Cave-Brown-Cave, Professor 142
C-B-C Engine cooling system 142–143
coachbuilders
  Alexander, Walter & Co 91, 112, 119,
    203
  BBW 89, 105, 177
  Bond 43
  Briggs Motor Bodies 121
  Brush Coachbuilders 31, 51, 52, 55,
    67, 70, 106–107, 180
  Burlinwgham, H.V. 91–92, 101, 106,
    128, 196–197
  Bus Bodies (SA) Ltd (Busaf) 102, 169
  Cravens Ltd 187
  Dodson, Christopher Ltd 26, 29, 39,
    43
  Duple Motor Bodies Ltd 59, 73, 89–
    90, 93, 112, 119
  East Lancashire Coachbuilders 71, 79,
    149, 150–151
  Eastern Coach Works 31, 105, 121
  Hall Lewis 46, 52
  Harkness 69, 75
  Jonckheere 132, 205
  Lincs Trailer Co. 94
  Massey Brothers 72, 96, 106, 162, 193
  Metropolitan-Cammell Carriage and
    Wagon Company (MCCW) 43, 46,
    52, 64, 96, 101, 164
  Mulliners Ltd 122, 129, 201
  Northern Coachbuilders Ltd 44, 106
  Northern Counties Motor &
    Engineering Company (NCME) 70,
    100, 105–107, 148, 157, 162, 192
  Nudd Bros and Lockyer 112

Park Royal Vehicles 52, 58, 70–72, 75,
    79, 83, 86, 96, 102, 107, 113, 148,
    159, 193
Pickering, R.Y. & Co. 106
Ransomes 39
Reading & Co. 113–115, 177
Roe, Charles H. 42, 68, 78, 80, 91,
    100, 103, 105–107, 145, 161, 179
Santus Motor Bodies 65
Saunders-Roe 96, 196–197
Short Bros 28
Stearne 16
Strachan 58, 106–107, 160
Strachan & Brown 30
Van Hool 132, 205
Wadham Bros 16, 118
Walmer 17
Waveney 55
Weymann Motor Bodies Ltd 43, 57,
    77, 105, 107, 159, 177, 192
Willowbrook Ltd 73, 81, 93
Windover Ltd 67
Coatalen, Louis 10
Cotal preselective system 53
Coventry-Climax 164
Cox, Ronald Edgley 81
Crellin Duplex 93–95
Cummins 167

Daimler Fleetline 136, 156
Daimler Roadliner 167
Daimler, purchase by Jaguar 156
Daimler-Knight (engine) 22
Dennis Brothers 13, 35
Dennis Loline 137

Deutz (air-cooled engine) 115
Dragonfly (aircraft engine) 14
Drop Frame Chassis 21

East Anglia Transport Museum 173
Elliot/Reversed Elliot axle 68

Gardner HLW engine announcement 85
Gardner, L. & Sons Ltd 46
General Electric Company 9
General Motors 8
GS model for London Transport 120–124
Guy as a coachbuilder 74
Guy Motors (Europe) Ltd formation 157
Guy Motors Ltd formation 11
Guy Vehicle Models
    13/36 Touring Car 19
    30cwt lorry 13
    Arab I introduced 57
    Arab II introduced 57
    Arab III (double deck) introduced 70
    Arab III (single deck) introduced 64
    Arab IV introduced 95
    Arab model introduced 49
    Arab UF announced 85
    Arab V introduced 158
    B model introduced 21
    BT and BTX models introduced 38
    C model introduced 30
    Conquest model introduced (original)
        45
    Conquest model introduced (revised)
        167
    FBB model introduced 24
    Invincible model introduced 45
    ON model introduced 26
    OND and ONDF models introduced
        32
    Otter model introduced 117
    Postbus 14
    Promenade 'Runabout' 16
    Seal model introduced 129
    Six-wheel chassis introduced 26
    V8 Car 17, 18
    Victory J introduced 169
    Victory model introduced 130
    Victory Trambus introduced 133
    Vixen model introduced (original) 54

Vixen model introduced (revised) 117
    Warrior LUF model introduced 125
    Warrior model introduced 125
Guy, Robin Slater 13
Guy, Sydney Slater 9
    letter to Commercial Motor 36
    time spent in South Africa 155
Guy, Trevor Maurice 13
Guy, William Ewart 9
Guy, Wolf model introduced 54

Hillman, William 10
Humber Company 9

industrial relations 25
introduction of 30ft, two axle chassis 81

J. Brockhouse & Co. 75
Jaguar 156
Johannesburg 'jumbos' 102
Johannesburg front 99

Lancia 46
Land Liners Ltd (sleeper coach) 30
Leyland Atlantean 136, 156
Leyland B15 Titan 153
Leyland Cub 120
Leyland Motors 35
Leyland Worldmaster 169
London Bus Museum 181
London Public Omnibus Company 29, 30
Lyons, (Sir) William 156

Meadows 4HDC330 engine 125
Meadows 6DC630 engine 65
Meadows, acquisition by Jaguar 164
Meadows, Henry, Ltd, profile 125

nationalization of transport undertakings
    80
North West Transport Museum 172, 192,
    195

operators
    Accrington Corporation 150
    Adelaide 76
    Aldershot & District 91, 93, 106
    Barton 46, 55, 58–59

Belfast Corporation 69, 75, 149, 163,
    176
Birch Bros 73
Birkenhead Corporation 71
Birmingham Corporation 26–28, 46,
    48–49, 95–97, 190–192
Black & White Motorways Ltd 92–93
Blackpool Corporation 51
Blue Line 75, 161, 196
Bournemouth Corporation 16, 76–77,
    109, 163, 175
Brisbane 76–77
Bulawayo 67
Burton-upon-Trent Corporation 23,
    51, 52, 67, 72
Bury Corporation 148
Cape Town 40
Central SMT 91
Cheltenham District Traction Company
    33, 45
Chester City Transport 162, 194–196
China Motor Bus 149, 170, 203–205
County Motors 151, 203
Court Cars (Torquay) 118
Danish State Railways 67
Derby Corporation 43, 80, 163
Devon General 107
Dodds of Troon 128, 198–201
Don Everall Ltd 91
Douglas (Isle of Man) Corporation
    122–123
Durban Transport 77
East India Tramways Co. 55
East Kent Road Car Co. 71, 110
Edinburgh Corporation 64, 103, 106,
    111, 180, 182, 184–186
Exeter Corporation 98, 193
Falga Motor Co. 94
Franky Tours 132, 205
Georgetown (Malaysia) 77
Gosport & Fareham Omnibus Company
    (Provincial) 105, 113, 177–178
Great Western Railway 25
Guernsey Railways 119
Harper Bros (Heath Hayes) 91–92,
    106, 161, 196
Hastings Tramways 39, 41, 176–177
Huddersfield Corporation 163

operators *continued*

Hull Corporation 76, 78–79
Hulley's 119
Johannesburg 40, 77, 102
Khartoum 67
Kitchen & Son 86
Kowloon Motor Bus Company 169, 203
Lancashire United 68, 91, 100, 103, 148, 187–189, 192
Land Liners Ltd 30
Leicester Tramways Department 31
Leybourne Grange Hospital 201
Lincoln Corporation 116
Liverpool Corporation 22
Llandudno Borough Council 54, 55
London Public Omnibus Company 29, 30
London Transport 8, 58, 83–84, 110, 120–123, 172–173, 180
Lowestoft Corporation 24, 31
Maidstone and District 107
Middlesbrough Corporation 103
Midland Red 107, 137, 180
Morecambe Corporation Tramways 28
Nairobi 67, 102
Newcastle Corporation 43
Newport Corporation 82
North Western Road Car 107
Northampton Corporation 179
Northern General 67
Norwich Tramways 28
Oldham 28
Phillips Coaches 201
Plymouth Corporation 179
Pontypridd UDC 100
Portsmouth Corporation 16, 62
Pretoria 77
Reading Corporation 79, 163, 175
Red and White Services 73, 89–90, 177–178, 185–188
Rio de Janeiro 22
Salford Corporation 28
Samuel Ledgard 86

Scottish Omnibus 112
Selecta Cars 132
Singapore Traction Co. 103
Societe des Chemins de Fer Vicinaux (SNCV) 167
South Africa 67
South African City Tramways group 169
South African Railways 134
South Lancashire Transport 42, 43
Southampton Corporation 52, 72, 88–89, 96, 107, 183–184
Southdown Motor Services 70, 98–99, 108, 160, 194
Southern Motorways 123, 174
Southern Vectis 33
Springs Municipal Transport 165
Swindon Corporation 57, 179
Teesside Railless Traction Board 163, 175
Tillingbourne Bus Company 123
UTIC 103
W. Alexander & Sons Ltd 67–68
Walsall Corporation 81, 157
West Bromwich Corporation 123, 173–174
West Pakistan Road Transport Board 163
West Riding Automobile Company 103, 137, 202–203
Western National 23
Western SMT 112
Wheildon (Green Bus) 65, 90
Wolverhampton Corporation 20, 21, 26, 28, 32, 38, 39, 53, 68–70, 76, 101, 151, 159
Yorkshire Woollen District 106

Perkins P4 engine 117
Perkins P6 engine 117

Rees-roturbo (electrical equipment) 40
regenerative braking 38
Road Traffic Act 47

Rolls-Royce B81 engine 134
Ruston & Hornsby (air-cooled engine) 116

Scammell Lorries Ltd 164
Science Museum 180
Scottish Vintage Bus Museum 178, 182, 185, 203–205
six-wheel chassis, campaign in Commercial Motor 36
six-wheel chassis, use in London 29
Southampton & District Transport Heritage Trust 183
Southern Railway 138
Standard-Triumph 164
Star 'Flyer' 34
Star Engineering Company 34
Stokes, Donald (later Lord) 164
Sunbeam Motor Car Company 9
Sunbeam trolleybus business, acquisition by Guy Motors 75
Swallow Sidecar Company 156

Tilling Group 8, 80, 137
Tilling-Stevens 20, 26, 38
Transport Museum, Wythall 178, 186, 190–192 8
transport through the Syzygies 56
trolleybuses, final home market deliveries 163
trolleybuses, new post-war range 76–80

utility bus bodywork 60, 61
utility bus developments 55
utility regulations relaxed 63

Vauxhall Motors Ltd 8, 49
Victory Airide 140
Victory model, air suspension developments 132
Volvo Ailsa 154

West Riding Omnibus Museum Trust 202–203
White and Poppe 13